W9-AYE-979

The Tea Book

by Sara Perry

photography by Edward Gowans

CHRONICLE BOOKS
SAN FRANCISCO

Copyright © 1993 Sara Perry and Judith Ann Rose
Photography copyright © 1993 Edward Gowans
All rights reserved. No part of this book may be
reproduced in any form without written permission
from the publishers.

Every effort has been made by the author to include
recipes that have not been previously copyrighted.
Should any such published recipes appear in this
book it is without her knowledge and is
unintentional.

Printed in Hong Kong

Library of Congress Cataloging-in-Publication Data

Perry, Sara.
      The tea book
   by Sara Perry ; photography by Ed Gowans.
         p.   cm.
      Includes index.
      ISBN 0-8118-0336-8
      1. Tea. I. Title.
   TX817.T3P47   1993
   641.3′372—dc20
   92-38967 CIP

Distributed in Canada by Raincoast Books,
112 East Third Avenue, Vancouver, B.C. V5T 1C8

10 9 8 7 6 5 4 3 2 1

Chronicle Books
275 Fifth Street
San Francisco, CA 94103

*To my mother and father, Martha and Elmer Wheaton,
whose loving kindness has made my life rich, and to Ron
Schmidt (1936–1992), who taught me the courage to look
issues straight in the eye, and the wisdom to know I didn't
need a watch to tell the time.*

Design and Creative Direction by Judith Rose

Edited by Catherine Gleason

Food styling by Sam McKean

Typesetting by Irish Setter

Carl Greve Jewelers of Portland, Oregon, has courteously supplied the dinnerware pictured throughout this book. Jeri Haber graciously provided the contemporary tea services from her private collection.

Table of Contents

Introduction

In the American West, mountain men treasured their black tea, which arrived in cannisters imported from China by way of Oregon. Tea provided warmth and stimulation, and their favorite, the smoky Lapsang Souchong, was the kind of manly brew they appreciated. In Europe, when twentieth-century philosopher Vaclav Havel was suffering in a political prison because he believed in democracy, he found his tea ration provided the one consolation and comfort he could count on. In California as a child, tea was a magical drink I shared with my godmother. At her kitchen table, just big enough for the two of us, we'd sit and share a pot of English Breakfast tea, which she drank plain, and I drank sweetened with warm milk and honey. After Gracie poured my cup, I counted the bubbles that appeared on the surface. Miraculously, I found dimes equal to the number of bubbles when I lifted my saucer and looked underneath. Tea carries different associations for different people, but its common denominator is comfort.

It is our pleasure to help you discover the best way to make a perfect cup of tea. We explore the many different types of tea, which, depending on your preference, will provide you with the palest and most subtle of green teas or with a tea so rich and golden it resembles amber. And we describe essential characteristics of the most popular and available teas, and the effect of climate, topography, harvesting, and production on your cup of tea. Tea has a mysterious and international history, and we bring you many of its fascinating episodes. Finally, we offer a varied collection of seasonal and cultural recipes that will perfectly complement your cup of hot tea or your glass of ice tea. Some of the recipes incorporate tea as a seasoning, and all embody the subtle, sophisticated, and comforting pleasures of tea.

THE *History* AND *Cultivation* OF *Tea*

*T*ea's discovery is lost among the folktales of wisemen. Chinese storytellers recite the legend of Emperor Shen Nung, the father of agriculture and herbal medicine, who lived almost three thousand years before Christ and taught his people the value of cultivating land and the wisdom of boiling water to make it safe for drinking. One day, while working in his own garden, Shen Nung noticed the leaf of a camellia-like bush floating in his steaming bowl of water. Sipping the concoction, he discovered a drink far more refreshing and exhilarating than plain water.

For the Japanese, the origin of tea arises from an act of atonement rather than discovery. Their central character is the missionary monk, Daruma, who brought Zen Buddhism from India to China and Japan. In 520 A.D., Daruma began a nine year meditation in a cave-temple near Canton, but growing weary after many months of staring at a stone wall, he fell asleep. Awaking, Daruma was so dismayed he cut off his lazy eyelids and threw them to the ground. It was there, according to legend, that the first tea plant grew, providing Daruma with an elixir which kept him alert during the remaining years of his reverie.

By the eighth century, tea was eulogized in Chinese literature and legislation. In 780 A.D., the poet, scholar (and one-time acrobat) Lu Yu wrote the definitive commentary on tea. *Ch'a Ching*, known as *The Classic of Tea*, and still read today, described how tea was cultivated, produced, and enjoyed. Politicians were elated to realize a new source of revenue was at their fingertips, and they levied the first tea tax just ten years later.

With each succeeding dynasty, tea evolved to reflect current society. During Lu Yu's era, the T'ang Dynasty (618–906 A.D.), tea enjoyed a golden age. The world's largest empire was a mecca for traders, and tea was a flavorful commodity. During this period, tea was introduced to Japan by Buddhist monks returning from pilgrimages to China. Pounded and shaped into molds, tea bricks were easy to transport, and the beverage was made simply by breaking off a chunk and popping it into boiling water.

During the Sung Dynasty (960–1280 A.D.), the refinements of tea culture blossomed in both China and Japan. Powdered tea and delicate porcelain came into vogue, and the first teahouses appeared. Many of the rituals used in the Japanese tea ceremony date to this elegant period.

Prized as a tonic and panacea, tea's shiny leaves were considered food by early Asian nomads. Some of the world's first energy bars were concocted by mixing tea leaves with salt, garlic, and dried fish, and the portable result made a handy form of exchange. After the social, political, and cultural upheaval of Kublai Khan and his Mongol relatives, the Ming Dynasty (1368–1644 A.D.) attempted to revive many lost rituals. The black, green, and oolong teas we are familiar with today were developed during this dynasty, and the teapot became an indispensable vessel for brewing.

As sixteenth century Portuguese, Dutch, and other European traders and missionaries began to visit the Orient, word of the beverage spread. Tea was introduced to England by the Dutch in the early 1600s, but remained the drink of aristocrats until the 1650s, when coffeehouses introduced tea as an alternative to coffee and hot chocolate. In 1657, Garway's Coffee House in London advertised tea as a cure-all, which made its cost easier to swallow, and rumors attributing Chinese longevity to tea drinking helped spread the gospel to health conscious Europeans. But, it was considered a man's drink until King Charles II's consort, Catherine, introduced tea at court as the fashionable breakfast drink to replace ale. It was also during this period that Russia became fascinated with the new beverage, which was brought by camel caravans trekking across Mongolia.

Tea came to North America in the midseventeenth century when the Dutch settled on the small island now known as New York. The neighboring English colonies took longer to embrace the drink. In fact, they didn't drink it at all. They boiled the leaves, and ate the lifeless vegetation with a little salt and butter.

Barely a hundred years after its introduction to Great Britain, tea had become an international commodity with tea gardens and street hawkers, but its popularity in America imploded due to an ill-conceived political maneuver. The British government levied a special tax on teas destined for the colonies, and the colonies protested with a boycott. As tea sales plummeted, the British tried to force the colonies to take the surplus, and, in a manner of speaking, they did. In December, 1773, the Boston Tea Party, one of many held in different ports, dunked the tea in the harbor, and set the stage for the American Revolution.

It was decades before Americans began to drink tea again. Now, at the end of the twentieth century, it has become an extremely popular drink, second only to cola when iced. Tea is a universal beverage: a staple in China, a religious tradition in Japan, the equivalent of a handshake in Morocco, and the Brits' eccentric way of telling time.

*Too Hot To Handle: In the scorching summer of 1904, an Englishman by the name of Richard Blechynden discovered **ice tea** quite by accident. He was attending the St. Louis World's Fair to promote Indian black tea, but no one was willing to try the steaming brew. Out of desperation the frantic gentleman poured the hot tea over ice, and to everyone's delight a quenching new beverage was invented.*

GROWING TEA: An old-fashioned bouquet of camellias and your grandmother's tea service have more in common than the sideboard on which they're standing. The tea bush and the camellia bush are kissing cousins, related by the scientific classification of genus. The familiar camellia plant with its shiny, green leaves and lovely, corsage-like blossoms is known as *Camellia japonica*, while the evergreen tea plant that supplies the world with its second-most popular beverage is *Camellia sinensis*.

A collection of Yi-Hsing-style teapots.

Native to Asia, the tea bush or shrub thrives in semi-tropical and tropical climates. Although its glossy, elliptical leaves grow quickly in a humid, jungle-like environment, the best tea grows above 5,000 feet, where harsher conditions encourage the leaves to mature slowly and develop complexity. Most cultivated tea is grown on large estates, plantations, or "gardens," but there are still postage-stamp-size plots, especially in China and Japan, where individual families grow enough for themselves, their village, and, when the price is right, export.

If left to grow wild, the tea plant can reach 30 feet in height or higher. (In the Yunnan province of China, there is an ancient tea "tree" that towers over the landscape at a hundred feet.) For commercial use, cultivated plants are pruned to waist height. Pruning encourages dense growth of the young shoots, called "flush," and makes it easier for workers to harvest the crop.

Even though a great deal of tea production has been mechanized, the young shoots destined for your teapot are still hand-picked. An experienced tea leaf plucker—usually a woman —can pick enough shoots in one day to produce nine pounds of finished tea, equal to 1800 cups of tea, or the annual consumption of a thirsty Englishman.

The number of leaves plucked from each shoot is one of the major factors determining quality. If the worker takes the top two leaves and bud, they will be used to produce a good to "normal" tea. The finest teas use only the flavorful top leaf and bud, while a coarse plucking grabs the first three, four, or five leaves on a sprig and produces a stronger, harsher brew.

With the variety of teas on the market, you might assume there are many different kinds of tea plants. Until the nineteenth century, it was believed that green tea was made from one species and black tea from another, but, thanks to noted botanist Sir George Watt, the different tea plants were identified as belonging to the same species. Nevertheless, types of tea differ dramatically, depending on climate, topography, soil, harvesting, and production. The next chapter explains how the leaves are handled once they've been harvested, what's different about each variety, why tea gives you a lift, and what's *really* in a tea bag.

CHOOSING TEA

When you buy tea from a supermarket, gourmet shop, or mail-order catalog, you're confronted with dozens of choices. How do you determine which tea you'll try next? Do you end up with the kind your mom used to fix whenever you were sick, or settle for the brand that's at eye level on your grocery store shelf? One thing is certain, understanding how tea is processed, recognizing the different categories, and knowing what goes into the various blends will make choosing your tea far more enjoyable and interesting.

If you were to try to brew a pot of tea with freshly picked tea leaves, you would face a somewhat bitter and watery drink. What gives tea its special character is the way fresh tea leaves are treated after they've been harvested.

There are three major methods of processing freshly picked leaves, and each results in a different category of tea: green, black, or oolong. What sets these teas apart from each other is the amount of fermentation that is allowed to take place. Fermentation is a chemical reaction (oxidation) that occurs between the air and the leaf's natural juices. However, unlike fermenting grapes, fermenting tea has nothing to do with alcohol.

GREEN TEA's delicate, unfermented liquor most resembles the taste of the tea leaf in its natural state. Indeed, green teas like Gunpowder and Pearl Dew are often described as having a light, slightly sweet, herbaceous flavor. To create green tea, the freshly picked leaves are first steamed to destroy the enzymes necessary for fermentation. Then, the pliable leaves are rolled, forcing the cellular structures to break down and release their aromatic juices. A gentle heating or firing follows, to reduce the water content, and the firing is repeated until the leaves are dry.

The last step in making green tea is grading—distinguishing the leaf's shape and age. The choicest grade is Gunpowder. Its young leaves are rolled into tiny balls that resemble BB shot. Other grades include Young Hyson (middle-aged leaves that can be rolled or twisted), Imperial (older leaves made in the Gunpowder fashion), and several lesser grades, ending in dust.

Green teas are mainly produced in China, Japan, and Taiwan. Although many of the steps are mechanized, you can still find handmade teas in specialty stores and in some Oriental markets. When rolling is done by hand, it's a tedious process. A worker goes over each of the leaf-laden trays two hundred times or more, rolling the leaves against the tray with his palms. How he rolls the leaves will determine whether the tea is twisted, curled, flat, or pellet-shaped. These shapes help to determine how quickly the tea will infuse with water and, eventually, how your cup of tea tastes.

BLACK TEA is familiar to anyone who has ever enjoyed the dunk of a Lipton tea bag, a spot of English Breakfast tea at a fancy restaurant, or a tall, frosted glass of iced Ceylon on a summer afternoon. Black tea's popularity surpasses all other tea in the Western world today.

The most refined of the three categories, black tea tastes the least like the natural leaf.

Instead of steaming the harvested leaves, the tea leaves are placed on large, drying trays and allowed to wither until they are limp. Depending on the type of tea, withering takes place either in the sun or in the shade. Then the leaves are bruised and rolled either by hand or machine—which gives the air and the aromatic juices a chance to mix. Since the enzymes and bacteria are still present (they have not been deactivated by steaming as they are with green tea), fermentation can begin in the humid, climate-controlled fermenting rooms. This fermentation/oxidation process takes just a few hours. Once the green leaves turn a coppery red—a color tea specialists say reminds them of an apple turning brown after it's sliced—the leaves are ready to be dried (fired) to stop any further fermentation.

*It's quick. It's fast. But what is it? Not surprisingly, it was invented in the United States. Developed during the thirties, it's **instant tea**. Pouring boiling water over dehydrated granules may save an extra three minutes in brewing time, and for those with a very low threshold of patience, it might be just the ticket. With lemon and fruit punch flavorings, assorted sweeteners, and preservatives taking equal billing on the ingredients list, instant teas are a chemist's fantasy come true.*

Unlike green tea, black tea is graded according to size, not quality. After the tea has received its final firing, it consists of a jumbled pile of whole leaves, broken leaves, bits of branches, and very small particles of tea dust. Mechanical or manual sifters with graduating mesh separate these pieces according to size, for sorting by size not only gives the tea a better appearance, it also insures an even brewing time.

The two main grades of black tea are *leaf* and *broken*. Sub-divisions of leaf grade include Orange Pekoe, Pekoe, and Souchong, each referring to a particular size, color, or texture of the finished leaf. The broken grade is also divided into still smaller sizes, which are ideal for quick brewing and tea bags.

OOLONG TEAS are treated much the same way as black teas, but withering and fermentation times are cut down. This results in a tea that evokes the qualities of both black and green.

Unlike black teas, oolongs are graded only according to their quality. The best is called Choice, followed by Finest to Choice, Finest, Fine to Finest, etc., a bewildering array of superlatives that ends in Standard. Since there can be many crops in one year, the quality of an oolong refers not only to the character of the leaf and how it was handled, but it also refers to the time of year it was harvested. For example, the best Formosa oolongs are grown in the summer months. They usually carry the Finest grade, while the grades of the winter harvest, when the weather can be quite unstable, are usually Good to Standard.

Oolong tea originated in the Fukien province of China, where it is still manufactured today, but among tea specialists Formosa oolong is considered the best.

SCENTED TEAS AND FLAVORED TEAS

SCENTED TEAS AND FLAVORED TEAS have been around since the first tea drinker decided his tea needed a little pizazz. By adding the sweet or pungent flavor of a fruit or spice, the fragrant scent of blossoming flowers, or, in the case of Lapsang Souchong, pine smoke, tea manufacturers are able to alter or enhance their tea.

Jasmine, chrysanthemum, gardenia, and magnolia are the most popular flowers used in **scented tea**. For centuries, making Jasmine tea has meant gathering fresh jasmine blossoms in the early morning, before they've bloomed. When evening comes, and the blossoms open their heavily scented petals, they are placed either beside or mixed in with green or oolong tea. After several hours, the dry leaves absorb the sweet aroma, and the entire process is repeated until the desired amount of aroma and flavor is absorbed. Today, this method is still practiced, but technological innovations such as hot air blowers and combining machines help the blossoms spread their fragrance. With more expensive teas, all of the spent blossoms are hand-picked out of the tea before packaging.

Flavored teas, such as Orange, Peach, Black Currant, and Vanilla, are fast-rising stars on grocery store shelves. The scent or flavoring in these specialty teas is sprayed onto the leaves, which are gently heated to absorb the flavoring. **Spiced tea**, such as Orange Cinnamon, Nutmeg, and Lemon Spice, have spices and fruit rinds intermixed with their leaves to give their characteristic flavors.

BLENDING TEA: After tea is produced and graded, it's shipped in aluminum-lined, plywood chests and sold by tea brokers to companies which blend, package, and sell it. You continue to enjoy the delicate bouquet of your favorite brand's Darjeeling, or the full-bodied brew of its English Breakfast, because the tea blender is doing his job. It's his responsibility to maintain quality and consistency by blending the teas in his inventory and creating the tastes you've come to expect, and he spends hours each day tasting tea. Unblended, estate-grown teas can be found in catalogs and specialty shops, but they tend to be expensive.

THE COMPONENTS OF TEA: No matter what kind of tea you drink—black, green, or oolong—each has properties in common that affect how you feel, and what you taste and smell. These components are caffeine, tannins, and essential oils.

Tea's pleasant lift comes from **caffeine**, a mildly habit-forming drug appearing naturally in many plants (tea, coffee, and cocoa to name a few). People who drink tea often boast to their coffee-loving rivals that their beverage has half the caffeine of that high-octane bean. Sorry folks, that's not the case, but you can still pat yourself on the back. By weight, a pound of black tea has twice the amount of caffeine as coffee. What's the catch? You make 200 cups of tea from a pound of tea and only 40 cups per pound of coffee. Green tea has even less caffeine than black. If you want to lower the amount of caffeine in your tea, be sure to read about caffeine under Tea and Health on page 33.

The color, pungency, and body of a tea come from **tannins**. Chemically, tannins have nothing to do with tannic acid, and are known as polyphenols. During fermentation, a portion of the tannins are oxidized and become water-soluble. This is what gives tea its distinctive color. The unoxidized tannins, those that are not fermented, give tea its pungency. Because green tea is not fermented and its tannins are unoxidized, it is pale and has less body than black or oolong, but it may be more pungent. On the other hand, fermented black tea gets its rich, amber color from the oxidized tannins, but because it may have fewer unoxidized tannins, black tea may have less pungency than green. As with much of life, generalizations don't tell the entire story. Tannin content also varies with the particular type of tea, and black teas tend to have almost twice that of green.

The **essential oils** give tea its aroma and flavor. With black teas these soluble oils are produced during fermentation. With green tea they're present in the natural leaf. When you brew a cup of tea properly, the caffeine, tannins, and essential oils interact and combine to make a tantalizing drink that, next to water, is the most popular beverage on earth.

Trick of the trade: Next time you see **Orange Pekoe** on a tea label, you can feel a little smug, because you'll know you've cracked the code. The name Orange Pekoe has nothing to do with a citrusy flavor, an exotic blend, or a far-away tea estate. It's the word used to describe a thin, twisted black tea leaf that often has a yellow tip. However, since you don't know where the tea was grown or how it was processed, this is a little like buying a loaf of bread wrapped in a brown paper sack labeled "sliced" without knowing whether it is whole wheat, sourdough, or rye. In reality, brands labeled Orange Pekoe usually contain a smooth, even blend of Ceylon teas.

TEA DEFINITIONS AND TASTING TERMS

Agony of the Leaves *refers to the unfolding of the leaves when they come in contact with boiling water.*

Aroma *is fragrance. It may also be called nose. Whatever the term, it's the perfume of the infused tea leaf, and it communicates your tea's freshness and personality.*

Body *is the sensation of heaviness and thickness as tea touches your tongue. Irish Breakfast, a blend of Assam and Ceylon, gives a strong, robust sensation as you sip it, while a Darjeeling lightly caresses your tongue.*

Bright *is the lively, sparkling appearance that's a trait of quality teas. It also refers to the coppery brilliance of black teas.*

Brisk *is the sensation on your palate of a lively, pungent tea.*

Congou *is a Chinese term for non-broken, black Chinese teas that require a great deal of skill to produce. For language lovers: the Chinese character for this term is the same as the character for the martial art, kung fu.*

Flavor *is the subtle relationship between the aroma, body, and pungency of your tea. The next time you enjoy a cup of Darjeeling, notice the subtle and delicate balance of aroma and flavor and its lingering aftertaste. In some cases, flavor can be determined by just one quality which attracts your attention. For example, it's hard not to be impressed by the strong, smoky aroma of Lapsang Souchong.*

Flush *is the new growth that appears at the tip of each Camellia sinensis branch or shoot. There can be several flush in a season, but the first flush of spring is usually considered the finest.*

Infusion *is the liquor obtained from steeping or soaking tea leaves, or other vegetation, in a liquid.*

Pungent *is the sharp, almost sour sensation or bite inside your mouth when you taste a tea with a high percentage of unfermented tannins.*

Self-drinkers *are pure, unblended teas with a strong, full flavor and have enough flavor integrity so they do not need to be blended with other teas.*

Popular Tea Types and Blends

BLACK TEAS

Assam's deep color and rich flavor make it an ideal tea whenever you want a full-bodied brew. Grown in Northeastern India (the world's largest tea-producing area), Assam is the foundation for many of the finest tea blends.

Ceylon, now known as Sri Lanka, began growing tea in earnest when a blight in 1870 wiped out the country's profitable coffee plantations. It was here that Sir Thomas Lipton made his fortune. Sri Lanka's mountain-grown teas, called self-drinkers (unblended), are among the world's favorites. Delicately flavored and bright in color, they can be enjoyed any time of day, especially in the morning with milk. These teas also work very well iced because they don't become cloudy when chilled. (See *The Perfect Ice Tea* under Recipes, page 42.)

Darjeeling is often dubbed the champagne of teas. Its bright, golden-red color is attractive in the cup, and its fragrant aroma reminds many of muscatel grapes. The finest of India's unblended teas, Darjeeling teas are grown on the slopes (1,000 to 6,000 feet above sea level) of the Himalayas, near Nepal.

Earl Grey's signature is bergamot, a fragrant essence made from the rind of a citrus fruit (*Citrus bergamia*). Not all packages of Earl Grey tea incorporate the same blend of black teas, or the same amount of essence. It's worth experimenting to find the subtle balance of flavor versus fragrance that you like best.

English Breakfast starts many a sleepy-head's day, and is especially good with a dash of milk. Once made from a self-drinking (unblended) Keemun, now its strong, full-bodied flavor often comes from a blend of teas from India and Ceylon.

Keemun, the most famous of the northeastern China black teas, was, until the latter part of the nineteenth century, a green tea. Today, a fine Keemun is often described in terms of a fine wine. Reminiscent of a hearty burgundy, Keemun has a complex aroma and a thick, full-bodied liquor that makes an excellent afternoon or evening tea.

Lapsang Souchong is the popular, smoky South China tea, recognizable the moment the tin is opened, or the first cup is poured. Its pungent flavor comes from withering the leaves over pine wood fires, or smoking them over pine fires while the leaves are drying. Lapsang Souchong was a favorite with Western pioneers and trappers, and it's equally pleasing at the office, served black, or with sugar and milk.

Orange Pekoe is not really a tea, but rather a *grade* of black tea. "Orange" refers to the color of the leaf's tip; "pekoe" comes from the Chinese word for leaf. Tea sold under an

Orange Pekoe label can be a black tea blend from any country, but with finer brands it usually means a blend of Ceylon teas.

Russian Caravan is a strong, full-flavored blend often consisting of China black and oolong teas. (Lapsang Souchong is a favorite in this blend.) Evoking the ancient trading routes that brought tea from the Orient to the Russian Czars, Russian Caravan makes a delightful afternoon tea.

Yunnan is a delicate Chinese tea from the southwestern province of Yunnan, where tea has been produced since the second century A.D. The long, golden leaves make a delicate tea that complements highly seasoned foods, and is delicious iced.

OOLONG TEAS

Formosa Oolong's peach-like aroma and fruity flavor is best enjoyed without milk, lemon, or sugar. Originally grown on the island of Taiwan by Chinese who longed for their native oolongs, Formosa oolong has surpassed the native oolong in taste and reputation. It is one of the few commercially grown teas still produced on family farms.

Pouchong is often used as a base for Jasmine and other scented teas. Technically, it is in a category of its own, because it is not fermented as long as an oolong. Pouchong comes from a Chinese term meaning "wrapped," and many of the Chinese pouchong teas are wrapped in paper while curing.

GREEN TEAS

Gunpowder refers to a Chinese grade of green tea that is rolled into small nuggets. Pinhead Gunpowder is made from choice young tips and buds. Because the leaves are tightly rolled, they stay fresh longer than other green teas. Tea-drinkers enjoy the pale-green brew with its slightly bitter flavor, and some like to watch the leaves gracefully unfurl in water. Said to be high in fluoride, Gunpowder tea may keep your dentist at bay.

Gyokuro is a highly prized, non-ceremonial Japanese tea also known as Pearl Dew. Grown in shaded gardens, only the tender top buds of the first flush are made into this hand-rolled leaf tea with its pale color and rich, herbal flavor.

Jasmine is a green or oolong tea enriched with the sweet scent of jasmine blossom. Depending on its quality, Jasmine can be the subtlest of fragrances or the foulest of brews. Because of its pronounced flavor, this tea complements richly flavored foods that can hold their own. (If you're interested in a more complete description of how Jasmine tea is made, see page 18 under Scented Teas.)

Matcha is the ceremonial tea of Japan. It's made from the same leaf as Gyokuro, but it is dried in its natural shape and powdered after drying. Very little Matcha is exported for sale outside of Japan.

WHEN IS A TEA NOT A TEA? When it's an herbal infusion. Technically speaking, only a beverage made from the leaves of one plant, *Camellia sinensis*, can truly be called tea. If that's the case, what is an **herbal tea**? Over the years, herbal tea has come to mean any drink made by infusing parts of an herb or plant with boiling water. In Europe this beverage is called a *tisane* and is the favorite of mystery detective Hercule Poirot.

The world of herbal infusions is vast, and its history is ancient. While this book focuses on only one plant, hundreds are used in herbal beverages. For thousands of years, herbs have been appreciated for their curative powers as an elixir and tonic and for their ability to make the water in which they're placed taste better. While tea refers to a beverage made only with *Camellia sinensis* leaves, herbal teas encompass a variety of plant parts, from leaves and flowers to roots and bark. Processed in much the same way as green tea, these plant parts are dried soon after harvesting to avoid any fermentation.

When you make a pot of herbal tea, follow the same basic rules you would for making real tea. The amount of dry herb you use depends on the herb's strength, but generally it's ½ to 1 teaspoon of dried herb per cup and 1 to 2 teaspoons of fresh. Depending on your personal preference, herbal infusions are usually steeped between 5 and 10 minutes.

Today's market of commercially available herbal teas continues to grow as people seek alternatives to coffee and tea. Like traditional tea, a particular herb can be a self-drinker, or it can be blended with other herbs to make a beverage that unites the flavors of them all. Tea companies are also developing new herbal beverages by combining teas with natural juices or sparkling water to make a drink that goes as well with meals as it does on the football field. (Herbal teas and juices are high in potassium, making them an ideal, isotonic sports beverage.) Listed below you'll find some of the many herbs used to make herbal tea with a brief description of their effects.

Basil may have your vote as one of the tastiest herbs in Italian cuisine, but its leaves also make a soothing infusion to help alleviate an upset stomach and nausea.

Chamomile flowers produce a comforting herbal tea that is perfect as a bedtime treat with a little bit of honey. A popular herb, chamomile is used as a base for many commercially blended herbal tea mixes. The plant also makes an aromatic ground cover for a garden path or sunny patch of ground. Every time you step on it, you'll perfume the air with a fresh, apple-like fragrance.

Dandelions, so popular with children, so unpopular with gardeners, are also an aid to digestion when the shiny, notched leaves are infused to make a pungent tea.

Fenugreek leaves were used as a food by the ancient Egyptians and its seeds are still used as an ingredient in curry powder. The hard, yellow seeds when bruised and boiled to make a tea are said to help cure the rather disparate problems of baldness and nausea.

Ginseng is legendary as an Oriental cure for the many ills of mankind. A beverage made from its root has an anise-like taste and is said to contribute to long and healthy life. It's also purported to be an aphrodisiac, so your extended life may be an active one.

Hyssop has been used as a medicinal herb since ancient Biblical times when it was used to heal open wounds. In the Middle Ages, it was used as a flavoring in cooking and added a bitter, minty taste to soups and stews. A chalice was said to "slayeth worms in a man" and to cure "evils of the mouth."

Lemon Balm grows like a weed in many gardens, but as a hot beverage its restorative effects keep you on the garden path. It also aids in digestion.

Lemon Verbena's relaxing effects make it a delightful bedtime brew. It's a sweet-smelling, lemony beverage that cossets the palate. But why not take it one step further? Next time, try making a strong infusion, let it cool, and add it to your bath water.

Mint, the ice cream of herbal beverages, comes in a plethora of pleasing flavors. My favorites are lemon mint and peppermint. There's nothing better to drink if you have an upset stomach.

Parsley may be your splash of color on an otherwise dull dinner plate, but the hot beverage made from its fresh leaves is a tasty way to keep your breath clean, your joints limber, and your kidneys working.

Rose Hips, the red-orange fruit of the rose plant, make a sweet, brilliant red tea used in many natural cold medicines. Especially high in Vitamin C—a single cup more than equals a crate of oranges—it's Linus Pauling's dream come true.

Sage was a useful drug in ancient Egypt. Today, people drink sage tea to help alleviate the flu-like symptoms of a bad cold. As the name implies, this tea supposedly keeps your brain sharp and your memory quick.

Thyme is a culinary herb that enhances the flavor of many savory dishes and is essential to a *bouquet garni*. Thyme's leaves and flowers also make an aromatic tea believed to help relieve headaches, coughs, and the common cold.

There are a variety of ways to brew tea, from the Mongolian practice of pulverizing tea leaves and boiling them with salted milk to the aesthetic Japanese ceremony of whisking powdered tea into a sea-green foam. Western tea drinkers follow the Chinese method of combining tea leaves with boiling water. While the method is simple and straightforward, there are several essential steps. Easy as they seem, they are crucial to a good cup of tea. On the following pages, each vital step is described in detail, along with some interesting information to help you make that perfect cup of tea.

▸ **Make sure your kettle and teapot are clean.**
▸ **Use good-tasting, cold water.**
▸ **Use the correct amount of the best tea you can buy.**
▸ **Use the correct amount of water at the right temperature.**
▸ **Brew tea for the proper length of time.**
▸ **Serve it fresh.**

MAKE SURE YOUR KETTLE AND TEAPOT ARE CLEAN.
The freshest water and finest tea can quickly be ruined if your utensils aren't spotless. Even though your kettle is only used for boiling water, it needs occasionally to be washed and dried since constant use can build up mineral deposits, giving any water you put into your kettle an off-taste.

Have you ever noticed a brownish haze on the inside of your favorite teapot? That's tannin residue and it adds a bitter taste to your brew. Washing your teapot in a mild detergent, or baking soda, and using a soft brush, sponge, or cloth to wipe out the inside will take care of the problem, but make sure any detergent you use is completely rinsed out. Otherwise, the delicate bouquet of your favorite Darjeeling will taste suspiciously like a pan full of soapy dishes.

USE GOOD-TASTING, COLD WATER.
If the water you use to brew your tea tastes good, you're half-way home.

When using tap water, turn on the cold water faucet and let it run briefly before filling your kettle. Tap water loses oxygen when it's left standing in water pipes for several hours. Let that flat-tasting water go down your drain, not into your kettle. And, if you think you're getting a head start on boiling water by using the hot water faucet, think again. It's a waste of time, water, and taste. Unless you have a customized, instant hot water faucet, the hot water has idled in the hot water tank for several hours before reaching your kitchen sink, so it too will taste flat.

In many sections of the country, tap water smells suggestively like a hard-boiled egg gone bad. If your water has been chemically treated or has an unpleasant taste, try bottled spring water. It vastly improves the quality of your beverage.

After you have placed your kettle on the stove to boil the water, it's a good time to preheat your teapot with warm water. When your kettle water has almost reached a boil, pour out the warm water in your teapot and add your tea.

USE THE CORRECT AMOUNT OF THE BEST TEA YOU CAN BUY. It takes **one slightly-rounded teaspoon** of loose tea for each cup. The first time you try a new tea, use a measuring spoon. After you've measured the tea leaves correctly, place the leaves in the spoon you're apt to use every day. That way you'll be able to gauge the right amount of tea and prepare the proper strength.

Often, instructions will call for an extra spoonful "for the pot." That's not a hard and fast rule. Many enthusiasts prefer using the precise amount of tea required for the number of cups they are making. The extra teaspoon simply adds extra strength. After you have measured the amount of tea you're going to use and placed it in your cup or pot, add the boiling water.

Unless the teapot has a built-in tea strainer, I like to use a stainless-steel, wire mesh tea ball to hold loose tea. I fill it only half full so the leaves have enough room to expand and the ball can be easily removed when brewing is finished. (I'll use two balls if I'm making a large amount.) If you put loose tea in your teapot, simply place a strainer between the spout and your cup to catch the leaves when you are ready to pour.

The Tea Bag Dilemma: While most guidelines discuss brewing tea with loose leaves, the number of tea drinkers using tea bags continues to grow. Over 50 percent of the tea consumed in the United States is made from tea bags, while in the British Isles the amount hovers at 30 percent. Other than collecting exotic tea tins and reading fortunes, why bother with loose tea?

It is well-worth the slightly onerous task of disposing of soggy tea leaves which, by the way, if you have a garden, are good for compost. Tea bags screen from sight one of the subtle pleasures of tea drinking. Enveloped in filter paper, the finely cut leaves or dust just lie sedately under the covers. But when loose tea and boiling water meet, it's a full-blown romance. Tea leaves come in a myriad of shapes, sizes, and textures, and all it takes is a little persuasive hot water to unwind and unveil their secrets. It's a performance worth watching, and it's always different depending on the tea you use. Most important, many tea drinkers believe that the taste of a tea is subdued when it's bagged, and that loose tea releases all of its aroma and flavor.

*Yankee Ingenuity: In 1908, Thomas Sullivan, a profit-oriented New York City tea importer, decided it was time to cut his overhead by replacing the large, sample tins of tea he sent to his retail customers with small, individual silk bags. Today, filter paper has replaced the silk, and it's safe to say **tea bags** are here to stay.*

On the other hand, whether at home or in a restaurant, tea bags offer no-muss, no-fuss convenience in today's world of fast-food eating. And, tea companies are responding to demands from knowledgeable tea-consumers by improving the quality of the tea used in their bags.

When purchasing tea bags, it's better to buy smaller amounts or individually packaged tea bags. (Not the best environmental advice, I admit.) The reason is that the finely cut tea leaves used in tea bags have a greater surface area and become stale sooner than whole leaves.

Whenever you purchase tea in bags, keep in mind that the best tea does not necessarily mean the most expensive. It is true that fine teas cost more, but it's also true that expensive does not necessarily mean top quality. Many tea drinkers pay a premium for those lovely, imported tins whose packaging proclaims their reputation, but well-educated American tea agents are buying directly from the same quality sources on the world market and selling their tea for less. If you take the time to learn about the tea you like, you can make an informed decision about the kind of tea you buy. Try to buy from a merchant who will answer your questions.

USE THE CORRECT AMOUNT OF WATER AT THE RIGHT TEMPERATURE. A frequent misunderstanding occurs over how much boiling water to add. In fact, many instructions skirt the issue all together. They simply say, "Add a bag or a teaspoon of tea leaves per cup of water." What's a cup? To many of us, it's the tall, hefty 8-ounce mug we use at the office. To others, it's the 4-ounce demitasse enjoyed after dinner. To the tea expert, it's **6 ounces** or, by United States measurements, 12 tablespoons or ¾ **cup.**

(Some experts specify 5½ ounces or 11 tablespoons.) For the purpose of convenience, we'll stick to 6 ounces. To be sure your pot of tea is as perfect as your cup, measure how many cups it takes to fill it.

The temperature of the water when you pour it over the leaves should be **212° F. That's a full, rolling boil.** Unlike coffee, which is brewed below the boil, tea leaves require high heat to extract their flavor. As soon as the kettle water reaches a true boil, bring your pre-heated teapot to the stove and fill it there. Don't leave your kettle boiling too long; the water will lose oxygen and the taste of your tea will suffer.

BREW TEA FOR THE PROPER LENGTH OF TIME. That doesn't mean dunking a teabag in boiling water until the water turns brown. Tea leaves need sufficient time to open. Depending on leaf size, that can be between three and five minutes. Even though the color of a tea is the first sign of brewing, its darkness doesn't necessarily reflect its strength. A perfectly brewed Gunpowder tea only turns a pale yellow-green, while an Assam or Ceylon tea brews to a rich brown.

The time it takes for tea to brew really depends on leaf size. The smaller the leaf, the faster the tea infuses. The smaller-leafed Assam and English Breakfast teas and the ubiquitous tea bag infuse within three minutes. The medium-sized Ceylon takes closer to five. The large, brown leaf of a China oolong, or the tightly rolled pellets of Gunpowder tea may take as long as six minutes. Using leaf size as a guide, you'll need to experiment with your own tea to find its ideal brewing time. Savor the aroma while the tea is brewing, but be sure to watch the clock. If you let your tea steep too long, tannin's bitter qualities will march forward and the tea will taste stewed.

SERVE IT FRESH. When it comes time to serve, either remove the tea leaves by lifting out the tea bag or ball, or strain into another warmed pot. Then give your tea a quick stir to blend the flavors and insure an even strength. Serve in cups rinsed with hot water, and savor.

To keep tea temporarily hot, tea cozies work well to insulate your teapot. If you're desperate for a long-term solution, think about buying a thermos just for tea. That way you don't have to worry about picking up the flavor of Juan Valdez's favorite Java.

Whether you like black, oolong, or green, whether you enjoy it plain or with milk and sugar or lemon, take time with tea. Remember, unlike the coffee you swallow in haste, tea is sipped at leisure. As a British friend, Amanda Baines Ashley, likes to say, "Tea is not about doilies and fine china. It's about looking after oneself."

MILK, LEMON, SUGAR, OR PLAIN? If well-prepared, your tea needs nothing more than you to enjoy it. Whether you add anything else is really a matter of taste and tradition. In China and Japan, people prefer their oolong and green teas plain, while the British serve their freshly brewed black teas with a pitcher of milk. In Russia, a dollop of raspberry jam makes the sweetest of teas, and a slice of lemon is often used to brighten the somewhat flat-tasting Russian tea.

As a general rule, you'll find oolong and green are best served plain, while brewed black teas often are enhanced by additional flavorings. The most commonly used flavorings you're likely to come across at a high tea, a cafe counter, or a kitchen table are milk, lemon, and sugar.

Milk's popularity in tea dates back to a seventeenth-century English custom. Up until that time, tea had been served in heavy pewter or earthenware cups. When porcelain cups came into British vogue, milk was added because it was feared that adding hot black tea directly into the delicate china cup would cause it to crack. This was not the case, but, like the porcelain cup, adding milk became a hard habit to break.

Milk reacts chemically with tea. One of its proteins, called casein, binds with tannins, giving your tea a smoother, less astringent taste. (Remember, tannins determine the color, flavor, and pungency of tea.) With the full-bodied, black teas from India and Ceylon, milk has a mellowing effect, and, some say, actually enhances flavor.

You'd think adding milk to tea would be a simple task, but entire essays and chapters have been devoted to the how-and-when. It all boils down to two choices: If you first pour the milk, then add the tea, they will blend without so much as a stir; if you add the milk afterwards, you'll have more control of the amount of milk you use. Also, and this is getting picky, your cup stays warmer—and so does the tea—if you pour in the hot tea first, followed by the milk.

You'll find it only takes a teaspoon or two of milk to flavor your tea. If you add more milk, it changes the character of the tea. The casein binds with all of the tannins, rendering your tea a milky soup.

If you run out of milk, don't think you can use real cream. It may come from the same cow, but it's no substitute. True cream doesn't have as much casein, so its effect is quite different. It doesn't bind and so cannot complement your tea.

Lemon has been used by the Russians for centuries as a flavoring for freshly brewed tea. Its use was introduced to the Western world, along with self-righteous modesty, by Queen Victoria in the late nineteenth century. The revered ruler of Britain discovered the fashionable and tasty flavoring while visiting Vicky, her eldest daughter, who was married to the Prussian King. While lemon complements the taste of scented tea, it will also brighten the flavor of a less hearty black tea.

If you enjoy using both sugar and lemon, add the sugar first and give it a stir. Otherwise, experts argue, the citric acid present in lemon juice may prevent the sugar from completely dissolving.

Sugar, honey, and even raspberry jam have been used for centuries to sweeten tea. In Russia, there is an old custom of holding a cube of sugar between your teeth and sucking your tea through it. Honey, the main sweet food of ancient times, is another popular sweetener. Its effect is the same as sugar. While many commercial honeys simply

add sweetness to your tea, others will impart additional aroma and flavor. The honey label will usually tell you the type of flower the bees harvested and what flavor you may expect to taste.

Although sweeteners are usually stirred into hot tea to sweeten the entire drink, I like the childhood habit of letting the sugar, honey, or jam stay at the bottom of the cup for a sweet surprise.

STORING TEA: If your college roommate brought you a commemorative tea tin from her year abroad, perhaps one celebrating Prince Charles and Princess Di's wedding, it's time to toss the tea and make the tin a button box. If you opened the tin right away, to celebrate the royal union with "a nice cuppa," the tea tasted as fresh as the romance, and retained its peak performance for about a year. If you kept the tin sealed, the tea leaves stayed fresh for an additional year. Alas, after that, both the aroma and flavor, like some marriages, began to disintegrate.

Although each type of tea has a different shelf-life, it's best to use any tea you purchase within six months to a year. Green teas are the most perishable, and begin to deteriorate within a year of harvest. Oolong and black teas retain their characteristics for several more years.

Keeping the leaves stored in a cool, dry, dark place is the best way to preserve their freshness. Avoid glass jars, which expose tea to light. An airtight tin is best. Another factor contributing to a tea's longevity is the way in which the tea leaf is rolled. Tea leaves rolled into pellets (Gunpowder and Imperial green teas) or twisted (like the black Yunnan) last longer than an open, flat leaf, because less of their surface area is exposed to air.

Whatever tea you choose, remember to treat it as you would any delicate spice. Keep it away from heat, moisture, and, of course, other strongly scented teas or spices.

TEA AND HEALTH: Over the centuries, tea has been considered a healthy beverage as well as a pleasurable one. Its therapeutic powers have long been glorified by venerable scholars and breezy copywriters. Lu Yu, the Chinese tea scholar, described tea in 780 A.D. as a cure for headaches, aching limbs, constipation, and depression. Today, if you search your city's natural food stores or Oriental markets, you're sure to find a tea touted for burning off body fat and cholesterol.

One reason for tea's curative powers may be strictly hygienic. In many cases, today as in ancient times, tea is safer to drink than water because it's boiled first, killing any disease-carrying organisms.

Even though the ill effects of tea are almost non-existent, the **caffeine** in tea is a topical issue for many tea drinkers. Tea does contain caffeine in moderate quantities. A naturally occurring drug, caffeine gives you that pleasant lift and acts as a mild diuretic. Research has yet to confirm any ominous diseases related to its moderate use, but if you're concerned and would like to cut down on caffeine, you're one jump ahead by choosing tea as your beverage.

All teas, especially green tea, contain less caffeine per cup than coffee. (See Caffeine under The Components of Tea, page 18.) If you want to lower the caffeine still further, there are two simple ways of cutting down: buying decaffeinated tea or **second potting**.

Once boiling water touches the tea leaf, caffeine begins to dissolve. After a 3-minute infusion, half the caffeine will have dissolved into the hot water. By removing the tea leaves (another reason a tea infuser is handy) and using them to make a second pot, you'll have effectively cut down even more of the caffeine. (You'll also have lost some of the aroma and flavor, but the sacrifice may be worth it to you.) If you use tea bags, remember, they are made with small, finely cut or broken tea leaves or dust, so the first steeping occurs within one to three minutes.

> **Question:** *How long does a fruit-fly live?*
> **Answer:** *14.5 days.*
> **Question:** *How long does a fruit-fly live who drinks Jasmine tea?*
> **Answer:** *40 days, according to Chinese researchers.*
> **Moral:** *Don't keep Jasmine tea around your fruit basket.*

Serving tea can be as simple as handing your friend a steaming cup over the breakfast table or as elegant as presenting tea to the Queen's Tea Master. Whatever the occasion, there are several implements that will make your task easier. Here is a survey of the basic essentials, with interesting tidbits and suggestions about how to choose the right one, plus a brief glance at customs and ceremonies.

TEAPOTS: For over three thousand years, tea drinkers brewed and tasted their tea by simply adding compressed or powdered tea to a kettle or cup. It wasn't until the Ming Dynasty (1368–1644 A.D.) that a teapot was considered necessary. As the Chinese began to use dried leaves to make tea, they found they required another container to hold the steeping leaves. Wine and water vessels were used for a time, but they often cracked from the heat of the boiling water, and their narrow spouts clogged.

In the early 1500s, the Yangtze river town of Yi-Hsing began to produce unglazed, red and brown stoneware pots which were able to withstand high temperatures, and soon wider spouts were in evidence. Except for their diminutive size—about the dimensions of a woman's clenched fist—these early teapots closely resembled today's teapot. Even the whimsical shapes of fruits and animals we associate with fashionable boutique dinner-ware found their way into the first Oriental teapot designs. To make tea using a Yi-Hsing pot, each drinker filled his own tiny Yi-Hsing vessel with tea leaves, replenishing the pot with boiling water after each thimble-size cupful was poured.

As tea found its way to seventeenth-century Europe, so did the teapot, and before long European potters were using domestic clays to imitate Chinese designs. At first the Dutch tried to adapt their traditional delft ware but found the teapots would often break if they weren't pre-warmed. The British used sterling, silverplate, or other metals, which solved the breakage problem, but, since metal is a superb heat conductor, the tea quickly turned luke-warm. The 1693 discovery in Staffordshire, England, of a suitable clay for making delicate and heat-resistant stoneware, solved a practical problem, but not an aesthetic one. It was not until early in the eighteenth century that Europeans discovered the materials and techniques required to reproduce the fine Chinese porcelains they so admired.

In the last four hundred years, the design and function of a teapot have changed very little. The same principles apply to a priceless Ming teapot and your favorite, worn and chipped, china pot.

When buying a teapot, make sure the lid is secure, and won't fall off when you pour. (It wasn't until the nineteenth century that someone wisely manufactured a lid with a small protrusion, or tongue, to slip under the pot's lip.) Check out the teapot's spout. If it's possible, try it out. There's nothing more maddening than a drippy spout. Hold the pot by its handle to see if it feels right in your hand and there is enough room between your fingers and the lid so your knuckles don't suffer. With a multitude of teapots from which to choose, from automatic models to teapots with built-in infusers, take time to see which one best suits your style. And, while you're at it, check out the **tea cozies**. These padded covers come in any number of patterns and shapes, and are used to keep the contents of your teapot hot. (Just be sure to remove the tea leaves before covering your pot, or you'll have a stewed and bitter brew.)

TEACUPS: Teacups were originally tea bowls, much like the ones you might find in an Oriental restaurant today. Eighth-century Chinese writer Lu Yu described the tea bowl in great detail, down to the glaze which looks best with a particular tea. (Lu Yu was fond of a blue glaze which turned red tea jade green.) The Japanese further adapted the bowl's design to reflect different seasons and aspects of their elaborate tea ceremonies.

In eighteenth-century England, British tea drinkers were enchanted with the shallow, handless cups that served the Oriental health drink, but it wasn't long before hot fingertips and the affordable price of tea convinced people to switch to a larger, handled version. Following the fashion of drinking coffee and possets (a warm, alcoholic drink made with milk), tea drinkers adopted a single-handled cup version, letting the double handle remain with hot chocolate enthusiasts.

Choosing your own teacup is a personal matter of taste. The most important thing is that it feels good in your hand, and pleasing to your eye.

KETTLES: While you can boil your water in any saucepan or soup pot, a kettle is a handy investment. Most kettles are made out of metal, and the best have a chromium-plated copper body. The same principles you use in choosing a teapot apply to a kettle. My favorite everyday kettle is a Russell Hobbs. Automatic and electric, this sturdy brand plugs in anywhere—a kitchen counter, an office supply closet, or the small table right beside your computer.

INFUSERS AND STRAINERS: When you use a tea bag, the intricate world of tea infusers and strainers is lost to you. To some, this may be a relief, but I find an infuser part of the reassuring ritual of tea.

A tea **infuser** is a perforated receptacle in which a measured amount of loose tea is placed. Known as a "tea egg" or "ball," this metal container is placed in the teapot before the boiling water is added. It's important not to fill your infuser too full. The leaves need room to expand as they absorb water. If you do decide to make a large amount of tea, don't overstuff your egg, use two.

If you are using loose tea instead of a tea bag, or a teapot with a built-in infuser, a tea **strainer** will come in handy to catch stragglers and give you a clear cup of tea.

TEA CUSTOMS AND CEREMONIES: Every country serves tea in a way that expresses its own culture. In **China**, a cup of tea is a customary way to welcome a guest. In **Morocco**, shopkeepers still greet prospective customers with a glass of sweet, mint-flavored green tea. In **Russia**, served with a slice of lemon, a dollop of raspberry jam, or a lump of sugar held between the teeth, sweetened tea

A collection of tea strainers and infusers.

became a comforting supplement to the one large, daily meal served in traditional Russian households. To make certain that there was a constant supply of freshly brewed tea available, the Russians developed their own way of brewing tea, using a **samovar**. This large boiler, or giant kettle, keeps water hot all day long. A small teapot filled with tea concentrate rests on its crown, so that a hot cup of tea is available anytime, by mixing a small amount of concentrate with hot water.

It was the **British**, or to be more accurate, Anna, the 7th Duchess of Bedford, who introduced the delectable custom of afternoon tea to the Western world. The nineteenth-century practice of eating an early breakfast and a late dinner made afternoons long and lean, and Anna solved this dilemma by serving tea with a tantalizing tray of gourmet goodies. Today, this tradition continues to fortify and delight middle-aged power brokers as well as the after-school, nursery tea set.

By far the most remarkable tea custom to be developed is the **Japanese tea ceremony**. Known as *Chanoyu*, this ritual has become an important part of Japanese culture since tea was introduced to Japan over 500 hundred years ago by Zen monks traveling from China. Once a ceremony reserved exclusively for men, it is now a ritual both men and woman are welcome to study and share. The Japanese consider the tea ceremony a refuge where spirit, man, and nature come together, where serenity allows knowledge to become wisdom.

Whether the ceremony takes place in a home or a separate teahouse, there are guidelines to nurture every aspect, from the selection of guests to the choice of food, utensils, and topics of conversation. The sprinkling of water around a host's entry gate informs guests that preparations are complete and they are welcome to enter. As they remove their coats and shoes, slip into the sandals and walk down the garden path to the teahouse, they leave behind the outside world.

Although there are different schools of theory governing the ceremony, every gesture by the host and his guests is part of a prescribed ritual. For instance, guests enter the teahouse's small opening on their knees as an expression of humility; the host or hostess, guided by centuries-old customs, places a small amount of powdered tea called *matcha* into a tea bowl and, using a bamboo whisk and water, whips it into a light green froth. Both simple and elaborate, the ceremony acknowledges the four principles of an enlightened life—purity, harmony, respect, and tranquility.

Many foods have been developed as traditional complements to tea. In the following pages, you will find recipes to accompany your tea, whether it is hot, iced, spiced, or spiked. You will also find sweet and savory recipes using tea as an essential ingredient. Finally for a pause that refreshes, there are recipes for making a tempting array of delicious tea drinks.

The Perfect Ice Tea

There's a reason 80 percent of the tea consumed in the United States is iced. A refreshing thirst quencher that doesn't add calories, it's a fine alternative to soft drinks and alcoholic beverages.

Here are two methods for making sure your ice tea is perfect every time. When you brew ice tea in the traditional manner with hot water, the tea will often become cloudy when chilled. If this happens, simply add a little boiling water to the chilled tea and give it a stir. If you want your chilled tea to be crystal clear, use the cold water method.

Don't be afraid to try different types of tea. Jasmine and blackberry make fragrant brews, as do many of the scented and herbal teas. To add variety, try a touch of sweet sugar syrup or a couple of flavored ice cubes. Because the cubes are sweetened with sugar, they tend to melt quickly, so if you are serving them, it's best to pass them on a bed of crushed ice.

Hot-Water Method

> 4 cups (1 quart) cold water, divided
> 2 tablespoons (6 tea bags) black tea
>   leaves
> Ice cubes

In a saucepan, bring 2 cups of the cold water to a boil. Remove from heat, and add the loose tea. Stir, cover, and let steep for 5 minutes. Stir, and strain the mixture through a fine sieve to remove tea leaves. (For crystal clear tea, strain a second time through filter paper—the kind used for making drip coffee.) Pour the strained tea into a pitcher containing the remaining 2 cups of cold water. Stir, and pour into tall glasses filled with ice cubes.

Note: If the tea becomes cloudy when chilled, add a small amount of boiling water to the chilled tea and give it a stir.

Makes 4 glasses.

Cold-Water Method

> 2 tablespoons (6 tea bags) black tea
>   leaves
> 4 cups (1 quart) cold water
> Ice cubes

Fill a large glass container with the tea and cold water. Stir well, and chill overnight.

If you use loose tea, strain the mixture through a fine sieve to remove tea leaves. (For crystal clear tea, strain the tea a second time through filter

The Perfect Ice Tea accompanied by Sugar Syrup with Scented Mint, Orange Blossom, and Lemon Zest Ice Cubes.

paper—the kind used for making drip coffee.) Refrigerate until serving time. Pour into glasses over ice.

Makes 4 glasses.

Variation: To sweeten or flavor your ice tea, try one or all of the following:

To make **Sugar Syrup**, combine 2 cups of water and 2 cups of granulated sugar in a small saucepan over medium heat, and bring the mixture to a boil. Simmer until clear, about 10 minutes. Remove from stove, bring to room temperature, and store in a covered glass jar. (It keeps indefinitely in the refrigerator.) Use in ice tea according to taste.

To make **Scented Mint Ice Cubes**, bring 2 cups of water and ½ cup granulated sugar to a boil in a saucepan. Add one 6-inch mint sprig, cover, and let steep for 5 minutes to infuse with flavor. Strain and chill until ready to use. Fill an ice-cube tray ½ full with mint water, and freeze until almost frozen. Add a mint leaf or sprig to each cavity, and add more chilled mint water until the cavity is ¾ full. Freeze until ready to use.

To make **Orange Blossom Ice Cubes**, combine 1 cup of fresh, strained orange juice and 2 teaspoons orange-flavored liqueur. Fill an ice-cube tray ½ full with the mixture, and freeze until almost frozen. Add an edible blossom or petal (choose from citrus flowers, lavender, scented geraniums, rosemary, roses, pansies, violets, or nasturtiums, to name a few) to each cavity, and pour in more chilled juice until the cavity is ¾ full. Freeze until ready to use.

To make **Lemon Zest Ice Cubes**, combine 1 cup strained lemon juice and ½ cup sweet sugar syrup, and chill until ready to use. Fill an ice-cube tray ½ full with the mixture and freeze until almost frozen. Add a sliver of lemon zest to each cavity, and pour in more chilled juice until the cavity is ¾ full. Freeze until ready to use.

Russian Tea

(Pictured on page 46.)

Although the Russian custom of holding a sugar cube between your teeth to sweeten tea has some appeal, I have yet to try it in the company of others. Here's another delicious tradition that's easy to swallow. In Russia, it is served in a clear glass cup.

> 2 tablespoons (6 tea bags) black tea
> (try a Russian Blend or Russian
> Caravan)
> 4 cups (1 quart) boiling water
> ½ cup Russian Whole-Berry Jam
> (see Note)
> 4 thin slices of lemon
> 4 large sugar cubes, optional

In a pre-warmed teapot, place the loose tea, or tea bags. Pour in the boiling water, and let tea steep for 5 minutes.

Meanwhile, place a well-rounded tablespoon of raspberry jam in each clear glass cup or mug. Strain the tea into each glass, and top with a lemon slice.

For your second glass, if you're feeling brave, try the sugar cube method.

Makes 4 servings.

Note: *To make* **Russian Whole-Berry Jam,** *strain ½ cup of raspberry jam to remove seeds. Warm jam slightly to make it easier to fold in the fruit and carefully fold in 1 cup fresh raspberries. If you need to use thawed berries, be especially careful when you fold the fragile fruit into the jam.*

Amanda's Tea Blend

(Pictured on page 79.)

It's 4 P.M., and for those lucky enough to be in Amanda Baines Ashley's Pearl District office, it is time for a brief interlude. Time for afternoon tea.

> ½ pound loose **English Breakfast** tea
> ¼ pound loose **Darjeeling** tea
> ⅛ pound loose **Earl Grey** tea

Place the loose tea leaves in a large mixing bowl, and stir until well blended. Store in a dry container in a cool, dry place. To use, measure one rounded teaspoon for each cup of tea. Serve plain or with milk and sugar.

Makes over ¾ pound or between 150 and 170 cups.

Dr. Mom's Fireside Tea Nog, Russian Tea, and Dr. Mom's Private Reserve.

Dr. Mom's Fireside Tea Nog

This soothing, tea-flavored egg nog is the ideal prescription for a hectic day. It's also a tasty and nourishing drink when you're feeling low.

> 2 tablespoons (6 tea bags)
>   Earl Grey tea
> 2 cups milk
> 3 tablespoons honey
> 2 eggs (see Note)
> ½ teaspoon vanilla
> Whipped cream, optional
> Ground cardamom or nutmeg,
>   optional

In a heavy-bottomed saucepan, combine the tea leaves, milk, and honey. Over medium-low, cook the mixture until it is hot and steaming, but not boiling, stirring often. Strain out the tea leaves, or remove the tea bags.

In a bowl, lightly whisk the eggs and vanilla. Stirring with whisk, gradually add the steaming tea milk to the lightly beaten eggs until they are well blended. At this point, you may wish to reheat the nog. Pour it back into the saucepan and heat over low, stirring carefully. Strain through a wire mesh, and divide between pre-warmed mugs. Garnish with whipped cream, and dust with ground nutmeg or cardamom.

Makes 4 servings.

Note: *Buy the freshest eggs possible. The government has issued warnings about using raw or slightly cooked eggs. I have never had a bad experience using raw eggs, but you use them at your own risk.*

Variation: After Dr. Mom has fixed this nourishing potion, she might as well relax with a steaming cup of **Dr. Mom's Private Reserve**. Place 3 tablespoons of rum or brandy in a pre-warmed cup. Fill with the Fireside Tea Nog, stir, and garnish with ground nutmeg. Just what the doctor ordered.

Raspberry Fizz, Catalina Citrus, and Hollywood Spritzer Sun Teas.

Catalina Citrus Sun Tea

Here's a quick way to brew tea, whether it's on the sunny beaches of California's Catalina Island, or on a sunny windowsill. The addition of fresh orange and lemon juice makes this a refreshing summertime drink.

3 rounded tablespoons (9 to 12 tea
  bags) black tea
4 cups (1 quart) cold water
3 tablespoons granulated sugar
6-inch sprig of mint
2 cups fresh orange juice
Juice of 1 lemon
1 peeled (with membrane removed)
  and seeded orange, cut into
  thin pieces
Orange, in half-moon slices for
  garnish
Mint leaves for garnish

In a glass jar, combine the tea, water, sugar, and mint sprig. Screw on the cap and shake gently. Place the jar in a warm, sunny location for 3 hours.

Blend the orange juice and lemon juice into the tea mixture. Strain the mixture through a sieve, and add the orange pieces. Refrigerate for several hours before serving with orange slices and mint leaves for garnish.

Makes 4 servings.

Variation: For thirst-quenching **Early Mint Sun Tea**, use 2 rounded tablespoons Earl Grey tea, and a sprig of mint, and omit the orange and lemon juice. Chill after straining the loose tea and mint.

To make a **Raspberry Fizz**, fill a glass ⅓ to ½ full of Catalina Citrus Sun Tea, and top with your favorite sparkling water, flavored with either raspberry essence or raspberry juice. Garnish with skewers of fresh raspberries and mint.

To make a **Hollywood Spritzer**, place 1 tablespoon of Cointreau in the bottom of a chilled glass. Fill the glass half-full of chilled Catalina Citrus Sun Tea, and top with an inexpensive champagne. Garnish with a strawberry.

Chainaya

In Russia, the favorite sipping spirit is vodka, and it is often infused with distinct flavorings. In this recipe, an aromatic tea is used to make a drink known as Chainaya.

> 4 teaspoons fruit-scented, loose
>   black tea leaves (e.g. Earl Grey,
>   Lapsang Souchong, Blackberry, or
>   other fruit-scented teas)
> ¾ pint (450 ml.) plain vodka

In a glass bottle with a cap, combine the tea and vodka. Cap, and let the mixture stand at room temperature for 24 hours. Strain, and store in the freezer. To serve, pour a small amount in the glass of your choice.

Makes ¾ pint.

Centennial Cheer

This strong and masterful brew will ward off a city chill or a country blizzard.

> 2 cups freshly prepared, hot Lapsang
>   Souchong tea
> 4 teaspoons granulated sugar
> 4 strips lemon peel, each stuck with
>   1 whole clove
> 4 cinnamon sticks (optional)
> ¼ cup bourbon or Irish whiskey

Make the tea. Meanwhile, warm 4 small mugs or glasses with hot water. Place 1 teaspoon sugar, 1 lemon strip, 1 cinnamon stick, and 1 tablespoon of bourbon in each mug. Pour ½ cup of tea into each mug and stir.

Makes 4 servings.

Black Currant and Earl Grey Chainayas and Centennial Cheer.

Portaspillini

These tiny "pin cushion" scones make a tasty biscuit for dipping. In this recipe, they are paired with two sweet sauces which can be enjoyed at breakfast or as a snack with your favorite tea. But don't be afraid to use them next time you serve a hearty stew—they're perfect for capturing the last few savory drops.

2 cups all-purpose flour
1 tablespoon granulated sugar
1 tablespoon baking powder
½ teaspoon salt
1¼ cups heavy cream

GLAZE
1 egg, lightly beaten
¼ cup milk

Preheat the oven to 425° F., and grease a baking sheet.

In a large bowl, sift together the flour, sugar, baking powder, and salt. Make a well in the center of the flour, and add the heavy cream. Stir with a wooden spoon until the mixture just forms a dough. (Don't overbeat the flour-cream mixture or the scones will be heavy.)

Dust your hands with flour, and knead the dough gently on a lightly floured surface two or three times. Roll out dough ¾-inch thick. Dip a small cookie cutter into flour, shake off the excess and push the cutter straight down to cut the dough into the desired shape. (If you twist the cookie cutter, chances are the scones will not rise properly.) Place the tiny scones on a greased baking sheet. In a bowl, combine the egg and milk, and brush over the top of each scone. Bake for 12 minutes, or until golden brown.

Makes about 2 dozen.

Serving Suggestions: *On a dessert plate, place several portaspillini and a small bowl or saucer filled with* **Strawberry Sauce** *(see page 86) and* **Lemon Curd Dip**. *To make the dip, combine ½ cup commercial lemon curd with one, 8-ounce container of plain lowfat yogurt. Chill. For a low-calorie alternative, use lemon-flavored yogurt. To eat, dip the portaspillini into one or both of the sauces.*

Jack's Whole-Wheat Scones with Brandied Sweet Cream

Even a Wonder Bread fanatic will love the taste of these whole-wheat scones. The addition of dried fruits makes for a hearty breakfast, especially when served with a steaming mug of Irish Breakfast tea laced with milk and sugar. The brandied sweet cream, reminiscent of a holiday hard sauce, adds a festive accent.

1 cup all-purpose flour
1 cup whole-wheat flour
3 tablespoons granulated sugar
¼ teaspoon salt
2 teaspoons baking powder
½ teaspoon baking soda
½ cup (1 stick) cold, unsalted butter, cut into small pieces
2 teaspoons grated orange zest
½ cup each, dried cranberries and golden raisins (see Note)
⅓ cup chopped dates
½ cup plus 2 tablespoons milk

BRANDIED SWEET CREAM
½ cup (1 stick) unsalted butter
¼ cup powdered sugar, sifted
1 tablespoon plus 2 teaspoons brandy

Preheat the oven to 425° F. and grease a large baking sheet.

In a bowl, sift together the all-purpose flour, whole-wheat flour, sugar, salt, baking powder, and baking soda. (If any of the whole-wheat flour remains in the sifter, add it to the sifted ingredients.) Cut the butter into the dry ingredients until the mixture resembles coarse crumbs. Stir in the orange zest, dried cranberries, golden raisins, and chopped dates. Add the milk, and mix with a wooden spoon or your fingers until the mixture just forms a dough.

Dust your hands with flour and knead the dough gently on a lightly floured surface two or three times. (Handling the dough roughly or too much will keep it from rising properly.) Form a ball of dough and cut it in half with a sharp knife. Take ½ at a time, and pat out the dough in a circle, ½-inch thick. Cut the dough into 4 wedges for large scones, 8 wedges for smaller scones. Repeat with other half.

Place on the greased baking sheet, and bake 12 minutes for large scones, 8 to 10 minutes for small scones.

To make brandied sweet cream, whip the butter in the bowl of an electric mixer until it lightens in color, and gradually add the powdered sugar. Add the brandy, and continue to beat until light and fluffy. (Grand Marnier is also an excellent flavoring.) Spoon into a decorative crock or small bowl, and chill for 30 minutes. Leave the butter in the crock, or form into balls, and serve at room temperature.

Makes 8 large scones or 16 smaller scones.

Note: *Dried cranberries can be found in most cooking stores or specialty markets featuring regional food products. If you are unable to locate a supply, raisins or other chopped, dried fruit can be substituted.*

Clear Creek Fruitcake

Until I tasted Marie Hein's fruitcake I believed in the axiom, "There's only one fruitcake—it just keeps getting passed around." But her fruitcake has changed my opinion: it's like everything you always liked to nibble on, in one tasty package.

Steve McCarthy, the owner and cellar master of Clear Creek Distillery, and Marie's brother-in-law, likes to slip a small serving in his day pack and take it cross-country skiing, along with a thermos of black tea—trail mix with a lift.

1½ cups dried pineapple, chopped
1½ cups dried apricots, chopped
2 cups dried pears, chopped
2 cups dried apples, chopped
2 cups dark raisins or dried
   cranberries
1 cup golden raisins
1 cup pear brandy (see Note)
3 cups all-purpose flour
2 teaspoons baking powder
1 teaspoon salt
2 teaspoons ground cinnamon
½ teaspoon nutmeg
½ teaspoon allspice
½ teaspoon cloves
2 cups walnuts
1½ cups hazelnuts
1½ cups whole almonds
2 cups pecans
4 large eggs, beaten frothy
1¾ cups brown sugar, firmly packed
1¼ cups applesauce
¾ cup melted butter, cooled
½ cup molasses
Pear brandy for soaking

Preheat the oven to 300° F. Grease eight 3½-inch by 6-inch loaf pans, or, substitute two, 8-ounce cleaned pineapple cans for each loaf pan.

In a mixing bowl, combine all the dried fruits. Pour the brandy over the fruit, and toss to coat the fruit. Let stand for 30 minutes.

In another, larger bowl, sift together the flour, baking powder, salt, and spices. Stir in the nuts. Add the brandy/fruit mixture and blend well.

Combine the beaten eggs, brown sugar, applesauce, melted butter, and molasses in a small bowl. Beat until the ingredients are well-blended and smooth.

Combine the egg mixture with the flour mixture, and stir well to evenly coat all the fruits and nuts with batter.

Pour the batter into greased loaf pans and fill ¾ full. Bake for 1 hour. The cakes are done when the sides begin to pull away from the edge of the pans and a toothpick inserted in the middle comes out clean. The cakes should be a rich, mahogany color.

Cool in pans for about 15 minutes, then turn out on a cake rack. When thoroughly cooled, wrap in cheesecloth that has been soaked in additional pear brandy. Cover with foil, and store in an airtight container or refrigerator until ready to serve. The cake is best after 2 to 3 weeks "aging."

Makes 8 small loaves, or 16 small servings.

Note: *Although any good quality pear brandy will do, Marie and I recommend Clear Creek Pear Brandy.*

Sunken Grape Cake

This handsome cake is the inspiration of Monique Sui, one of Oregon's best pastry chefs and co-owner of Zefiro in Northwest Portland. The not-too-sweet almond base makes it ideal as a breakfast cake or afternoon refreshment, served with tea and sherry. Any seedless grape will do, but I prefer to use a purple Concord because of its deep, rich color.

> ½ pound unsalted butter, at room
>   temperature
> 1¼ cups granulated sugar
> 3 eggs, at room temperature
> Grated zest of 1 lemon
> 1 teaspoon almond extract
> 1 cup all-purpose flour
> 1 cup finely ground, toasted almonds
> 2 teaspoons baking powder
> 1 to 2 cups seedless grapes

Preheat the oven to 350° F. Butter and flour a 9-inch springform pan or a tube pan.

Cream the butter with the sugar until light and fluffy. Add the eggs one at a time, blending thoroughly after each addition. Beat in the lemon zest and the almond extract.

Mix together the flour, ground almonds, and baking powder. Stir the dry ingredients into the butter and egg mixture until just blended. Spoon into the prepared pan, and smooth the batter. Distribute the grapes over the batter in a single layer and press down lightly.

Bake 50 to 60 minutes until a toothpick comes out clean. Cool for 10 minutes, and unmold onto a wire rack. Dust lightly with powdered sugar before serving.

Makes 1 cake; serves 8 to 10 easily.

Chocolate Coco, Lemon Oatmeal, and Ginger Shortbread Cookies.

Chocolate Coco Cookies

With a hint of cinnamon, these triple-rich chocolate cookies are an ideal complement to other tea-time cookies.

> 2 ounces (2 squares) semi-sweet chocolate
> 2 cups all-purpose flour
> ½ cup Dutch-processed cocoa
> 1 teaspoon baking powder
> ½ teaspoon cinnamon
> ¼ teaspoon salt
> ½ cup unsalted butter
> 1 cup granulated sugar
> 1 egg, lightly beaten
> 3 ounces semi-sweet chocolate, melted

Melt the chocolate over a double boiler or in the microwave, and set aside to cool slightly.

Sift together the flour, cocoa, baking powder, cinnamon, and salt. Set aside. In the bowl of an electric mixer, cream the butter and sugar until light and fluffy. Beat in the egg, and slowly add the melted chocolate until well blended. Slowly beat in the dry ingredients until a dough is formed. Shape the dough into a square or triangular log, 1½ inches in diameter. Refrigerate for at least 2 hours, or overnight.

Preheat oven to 350° F., and grease baking sheets.

Remove the dough from the refrigerator, and cut with a sharp knife into ¼-inch-thick slices. Cut the individual slices into shapes with a cookie cutter. (The excess dough will not reform easily to make a smooth cookie, but will make a tasty free-form cookie when several pieces of the excess dough are pinched together.) Place the shaped dough on a greased cookie sheet, and bake for 7 to 10 minutes, or until just set. Cool on a wire rack.

Using the tines of a fork, a plastic bag with a small hole cut in one corner, or a pastry bag fitted with a fine point, pipe the melted chocolate over the cookies. Do not move the cookies until the chocolate has set.

Makes approximately 4 dozen.

Variation: For a softer cookie, slice the chilled dough into ½-inch-thick slices and place on greased cookie sheets. Bake the cookies for 10 minutes, or until just set. Proceed as directed.

Lemon Oatmeal Cookies

During a visit to the Portland Art Museum, I was treated to one of these cookies by museum volunteer Myrthle Griffin. I don't remember the exhibits, but I'll never forget these cookies. Their lemony flavor goes especially well with a cup of freshly brewed black tea (Assam or Dragonmoon are my favorites). This is one of those recipes that can easily be halved. These cookies may become your family's favorite.

> 2 cups all-purpose flour
> 1 teaspoon baking soda
> ¼ teaspoon salt
> 2 cups (4 sticks) unsalted butter (see Note)
> 2 cups granulated sugar
> 2 teaspoons lemon extract
> ½ teaspoon minced lemon zest
> 3 cups old-fashioned rolled oats

Preheat oven to 350° F.

Sift the flour, baking soda, and salt. Set aside.

In the bowl of an electric mixer, combine the butter and sugar. Beat until creamy white, for 8 to 10 minutes. With the mixer on low speed, add the lemon extract and lemon zest. Slowly add the sifted flour mixture until completely blended. Stir in the oats until blended.

Drop by teaspoonfuls on an ungreased cookie sheet, and bake for 10 minutes until very lightly golden. Let the cookies cool on the baking sheet.

Makes approximately 30 cookies.

Note: This recipe should be made with real butter.

Ginger Shortbread

Nuggets of crystallized ginger embedded in semi-sweet chocolate give these buttery shortbreads a pungent taste. This is the ideal cookie to serve on a summer's afternoon with a cup of Darjeeling, or on a stormy night by the fire, with a steaming Russian blend.

DOUGH
¼ **cup granulated sugar**
1¼ **cups all-purpose flour**
3 **tablespoons cornstarch**
2 **teaspoons ground ginger**
¾ **teaspoon freshly grated ginger root**
½ **cup (1 stick) plus 2 tablespoons
    softened butter, cut into chunks**

FROSTING
2 **squares (2 ounces) semi-sweet
    chocolate**
¼ **cup minced, crystallized ginger
    (see Note)**

Preheat the oven to 325° F.

In a mixing bowl, combine the sugar, flour, cornstarch, ground ginger, and freshly grated ginger. Add the butter, and work the mixture with your fingertips or pastry blender until it is crumbly and forms a coarse meal. Press the mixture into a large, firm ball.

Pat evenly into an ungreased 8-by-8-inch baking pan, and pierce the dough all over with fork tines. Bake for 40 minutes, or until golden. Immediately cut into desired shapes in the pan and allow them to cool slightly. Remove the shortbread, and cool completely on a wire rack.

To make frosting, melt the chocolate in the microwave or in a double-boiler. Place the melted chocolate in a small bowl.

To frost the cookies, dust the crumbs off each cookie with a pastry brush, and then dip the edge of each cookie into the melted chocolate.

Sprinkle with crystallized ginger, and place on a wire rack until the chocolate has set.

Makes 18 cookies.

Note: Crystallized ginger is available in the spice section of most supermarkets.

Cashew Shortbread

(Pictured on page 88.)

Here's another tasty variation for shortbread. Although cashews are rarely used in cookie recipes, they give a delicate scent and flavor to this buttery cookie.

    1 cup salted cashews
    1 cup all-purpose flour
    1 scant cup powdered sugar
    ¼ cup cornstarch
    ¾ cup (1½ sticks) softened butter
    1 to 2 teaspoons granulated sugar

Preheat the oven to 325° F.

Using the steel blade of your food processor, whirl the cashews and flour with several on-off actions for about 20 seconds. Add the powdered sugar and cornstarch, and process for 10 seconds more.

Place the cashew mixture in a large bowl. Place the butter in the bowl, and, with your fingertips or a pastry blender, work the mixture until it is crumbly and forms a coarse meal. Press the mixture into a large, firm ball.

Pat evenly into an ungreased 9-inch cake pan. Pierce the dough all over with fork tines. Bake for 40 minutes, or until golden. Immediately sprinkle granulated sugar over the surface and use a sharp knife to cut into desired shapes. Allow shortbread to cool for 10 minutes in the pan.

Remove the shortbread to a wire rack to cool completely.

Makes 12 shortbread cookies.

Chinese Vendor Tea Eggs and Tea-Smoked Chicken Wings.

Chinese Vendor Tea Eggs

In the Orient, tea eggs are often sold by street vendors as a tasty snack. Their unusual appearance makes them a clever addition to any picnic. Dusted with a combination of toasted sesame seeds and coarse salt, they make an excellent hors d'oeuvre.

> 3 to 4 cups water
> 6 to 10 eggs
> 2 tablespoons (4 tea bags) black tea
> leaves
> 2 teaspoons 5-fragrance spice
> powder (see Variation)
> 1 tablespoon coarse salt

In a pot, cover the eggs with cold water and bring to a boil. Simmer for 12 minutes. Remove from heat, and reserve the water.

Place the eggs in cold water until they can be easily handled. With the back of a spoon, lightly tap each shell all over until it is covered with a cobweb of cracks.

In the same pot, bring the reserved water (which should be 3 to 4 cups) to a boil. Add the tea leaves, 5-fragrance spice, salt, and eggs. Simmer covered for an hour. Remove the pot from the heat and continue to let the eggs soak covered for 30 minutes. Remove the eggs from the water, and allow to cool. To serve, shell the eggs and halve them lengthwise or quarter them. Their flavor is best enjoyed within 24 hours.

Makes 6 to 10 eggs.

Variation: Substitute Jasmine tea or light soy sauce for the black tea, and the peel of an orange for the 5-fragrance spice powder. (Use a vegetable peeler to peel the orange the same way you would peel an apple. Try not to take any of the white pith.)

Tea-Smoked Chicken Wings

Smoking with tea is a traditional Chinese approach to preparing chicken. To the Western eye, the darkened skin resembles Cajun-style cuisine. These flavorful, bite-size chicken wings make a delicious appetizer when served plain, or with your favorite mustard, peanut, or teriyaki sauce.

> 3 pounds chicken wings (16 wings)
> 3 cloves garlic
> 1 tablespoon grated ginger root
> 1 tablespoon honey
> ¾ cup soy sauce
> ½ cup sherry
> 1 cup brown sugar
> 1 cup loose Lapsang Souchong
> Sesame seeds as garnish

Using a knife, separate the mini drumstick end of the wing, and slice through between the joints. Cut the wing tip off, and discard. (Any good butcher will do this for you.) Wash the chicken thoroughly, and pat dry.

Using the metal blade of your processor, finely chop the garlic. Add the grated ginger root, honey, soy sauce, and sherry, processing for 20 seconds to blend. Pour the marinade in a 9-by-13-inch baking pan, and add the chicken wings. With a spoon, drizzle the marinade over all the wings. Cover and refrigerate for at least 2 hours, rotating the chicken wings at least once.

To smoke chicken, choose a heavy steel or cast-iron roasting pan or skillet with a tight fitting lid. Line the bottom of the pan with heavy duty aluminum foil. Sprinkle the brown sugar and tea on top of the foil. Place a cake rack in the skillet, over the sugar and tea mixture, and arrange the chicken wings on the rack. Cover the pan or skillet with a lid (or heavy aluminum foil if the lid does not fit snugly). Turn on your kitchen exhaust fan. Turn the burner on high, and leave chicken on high heat for 30 minutes (see Note). Do not remove the lid to check. Turn off the heat after 30 minutes, and keep the chicken covered for another 20 minutes. Smoked chicken will keep for several days if well wrapped and refrigerated.

Serves 6 to 8 as an appetizer.

Note: *As with any recipe requiring a dish to be cooked at high heat, use caution. Since this dish does produce smoke, it is imperative to use your kitchen exhaust fan, and to have a pan or skillet with a tight fitting lid.*

Rogue River Cheeseburgers

This interesting combination of flavors tastes great, especially with a tall glass of strong ice tea. The astringent, palate-cleansing qualities of ice tea make it an ideal drink for such full-bodied recipes.

1½ pounds lean ground beef
½ cup (approximately 4½ ounces) blue cheese, finely crumbled
1 teaspoon freshly ground coarse black pepper, divided
¼ cup freshly squeezed lemon juice
1 tablespoon minced parsley
4 homemade buns or rolls
Unsalted butter or homemade mayonnaise
1 large ripe tomato, sliced
1 sweet onion, sliced
Lettuce

Preheat the broiler or prepare the barbecue.
In a large bowl, gently mix the lean ground beef and blue cheese until blended. (Over-handling creates a dense, heavy-textured patty.) Shape into four patties, each 4 inches in diameter. Place on a greased rack, and top each patty with ¼ teaspoon ground pepper pressed in firmly. Broil or barbecue to your liking.
While the patties are cooking, combine the lemon juice and parsley in a small bowl, and set aside. Toast the buns and spread each side with butter or mayonnaise while still warm.
Place each patty on a bun. Drizzle 1 teaspoon of the lemon-parsley juice on each patty. Top with sliced tomato, onion, lettuce, and serve.

Makes 4 servings.

Summer Salad

Chilled or at room temperature, this colorful salad tastes especially refreshing on a summer's evening. Cooking the rice in freshly brewed orange spice tea gives a delicious aroma to the rice, and your kitchen.

1 medium orange
1 small lemon
6 tablespoons corn oil
1 tablespoon white wine or rice wine vinegar
½ pound small, peeled, cooked shrimp
2 cups freshly brewed orange spice tea
1 cup long grain, white rice
½ cup currants
1 medium red apple (unpeeled), cut in chunks
1 medium green apple (unpeeled), cut in chunks
12 to 14 snow peas, sliced (ends and strings removed)
3 green onions, thinly sliced
Butter or Boston lettuce leaves

With a zester, remove 2 tablespoons of zest from the orange and ½ tablespoon zest from the lemon. Set aside. Cut the orange in half, and squeeze 3 tablespoons of juice into a small bowl. Cut the lemon in half, and squeeze 2 tablespoons of juice into the bowl.

To make dressing, combine the orange juice, lemon juice, corn oil, vinegar, and reserved lemon zest in a quart jar with a lid. Screw the lid on, and shake the jar to blend the ingredients. Carefully add the shrimp, and toss lightly by screwing on the lid and inverting the jar several times. Set aside in the refrigerator.

In a 2-quart saucepan, bring the tea to a boil. Gradually add the rice and currants. Cover, reduce the heat, and simmer for 20 minutes. Remove from heat, and let cool to room temperature.

In a salad bowl, combine the red and green apples, the sliced snow peas, and green onions. Add the shrimp and dressing, and mix lightly. Add the cooked rice and currant mixture, and the reserved orange zest. Toss gently, and place individual servings on Butter or Boston lettuce leaves.

Serves 4 to 6.

Lapsang Souchong Sea Scallops

Larry Kirkland, one of the most inventive cooks I know, developed this delicious recipe for marinating sea scallops in an aromatic brew of Lapsang Souchong tea. The smoky flavor gives the scallops a distinctive flavor. Larry prefers sea scallops for this recipe, because bay scallops tend to turn rubbery when cooked for the required length of time.

14 cups water, divided
1 cup Lapsang Souchong tea leaves
½ pound sea scallops
6 to 8 medium zucchini
3 medium oranges
3 tablespoons butter
Coarse salt
Freshly ground pepper
Sliced and peeled orange for garnish
Green onion for garnish

In a saucepan, bring 6 cups of water to boil and add the loose tea leaves. Cover with a tight-fitting lid, and steep for 5 minutes. Strain the tea, and set aside in the refrigerator to cool.

In a glass baking dish, marinate the sea scallops for 30 minutes in enough cooled tea to cover scallops. With a slotted spoon, remove the scallops, and pat dry on paper towels. Reserve the tea marinade for later use.

With a zester, strip long strings from the zucchini. Make the strips as long as you can. Keep repeating until you get to the seed-filled center. (A medium zucchini should yield about ¾ cup loosely packed zucchini.) Set aside.

With the same zester, strip the orange skins into long "spaghetti" strings. Place the orange strings in a pot containing the remaining 8 cups of salted water. Bring the pot of water to a boil.

Meanwhile, in a 12-inch soup kettle, wok, or skillet, pour in the reserved tea marinade. Place a steamer rack (or jerry-rig a cake rack) in the skillet, making sure the rack does not touch the liquid. Bring the tea to a full boil. Place the scallops on the rack, cover with a tight lid, and steam for 7 minutes, or until just done. Remove the scallops and place on a warm platter.

Add the zucchini spaghetti to the boiling orange spaghetti, and cook for 45 seconds, or until the zucchini is just hot. Drain the zucchini and orange spaghetti, and toss with butter.

To assemble, place a portion of the zucchini and orange spaghetti on each of 6 warmed plates. Divide the scallops among the plates. Sprinkle with coarse salt and freshly ground pepper. If desired, garnish with orange and thin strips of green onion.

Makes 6 servings (as an appetizer).

Tea Sandwich Classics

Whenever Oregon restaurant critic and conversationalist, Lisa Shara Hall, has friends in for tea, it becomes a formal occasion. Her tea sandwiches are intentionally uncomplicated so as not to compete with good tea and rich pastries. Her guidelines make the task simple.

GUIDELINES

▸ Use thin-sliced white and/or whole wheat bread. An average 2-pound loaf will yield 10 to 12 regular sandwiches, which can be cut into 40 to 48 squares or 30 to 36 fingers.

▸ Always spread each piece of bread with butter, cream cheese, or a combination of the two. This seals the filling and prevents the sandwich from becoming soggy. To adequately cover 10 to 12 regular sandwiches, you will need ¾ cup.

▸ Keep fillings simple. You will need 1½ cups of soft, spreadable filling for 10 to 12 sandwiches; 2 or more cups for coarser fillings; and ¾ pound of sliced meats.

▸ To keep the bread from drying out, cover the slices with plastic wrap or damp cloth while you make the sandwiches.

▸ Vary the shapes of the sandwiches by using cookie cutters.

▸ Roll edges of trimmed sandwiches in minced parsley or chives. (It's easier to roll round shapes than angles.)

Smoked Salmon Sandwich Filling

½ cup (1 stick) unsalted butter, softened
½ cup cream cheese, softened
¾ pound thinly sliced, smoked salmon
1 bunch fresh dill

Spread one piece of bread with unsalted butter. Spread another with cream cheese. Place a thin layer of salmon on the bread. Top with a sprig or two of dill. Top with other piece of bread, spread side down. Trim crusts, and cut into 2 sandwiches, or cut with cookie cutter.

Makes enough filling for approximately 10 regular sandwiches.

Smoked Turkey Sandwich Filling

¾ pound thinly sliced hickory-smoked turkey
½ to ¾ cup unsalted butter, softened, to bind
Dijon-style mustard, to taste
Heavy cream, to bind

With a sharp knife, finely chop the turkey. In a small bowl, combine the turkey, butter, mustard to taste, and enough cream to make a creamy filling. Lightly spread the filling on one slice of brown or rye bread. Top with another piece, spread side down. Trim crusts, and cut as desired.

Makes enough filling for approximately 10 regular sandwiches.

Tea Sandwiches: Smoked Salmon, Egg Salad, Smoked Turkey, Watercress, Cucumber, and Cottage Cheese with Carrot.

Watercress Sandwich Filling
(Pictured on page 73.)

> 1 large bunch watercress (about 30 stems)
>
> **BUTTER SPREAD**
> 1 cup (2 sticks) unsalted butter, softened
> 2 to 3 teaspoons heavy cream, to bind
> Dijon mustard, to taste
> Squeeze of lemon juice
> Salt and pepper, to taste

Remove the stems, and wash and dry the watercress. In a small bowl, combine and blend the butter-spread ingredients. Spread each slice of bread with a layer of butter mixture. On one slice, place a thin layer of cress. Top with another piece of bread, spread side down. Trim crusts, and cut as desired.

Makes enough filling for approximately 10 regular sandwiches.

Cucumber Sandwich Filling
(Pictured on page 73.)

> 3 to 4 small, pickling-type cucumbers, or 1 long, English-style cucumber
> Salt
> Unsalted butter, softened
> Freshly ground white pepper, to taste
> Softened cream cheese

Peel cucumber, and slice as thinly as possible. Lightly salt the slices, and place in a colander to drain, weighted with a plate, for at least an hour.

Butter one side of bread, place one layer of cucumbers on top, and sprinkle with pepper. Spread cream cheese on other slice, and place on top of cukes, spread side down.

Makes enough filling for approximately 10 regular sandwiches.

Cottage Cheese and Carrot Sandwich Filling
(Pictured on page 73.)

> 1 cup (8 ounces) small curd cottage cheese
> 1 medium carrot, peeled and finely grated
> ¼ cup chopped, toasted walnuts
> 2 tablespoons honey, or to taste
> Unsalted butter, softened

In a small bowl, combine and blend the cottage cheese, grated carrot, walnuts, and honey. Spread piece of bread with butter. Then spread filling on top. Top with another piece of bread, butter side down. Trim as desired.

Makes enough filling for approximately 10 regular sandwiches.

Egg Salad Sandwich Filling

(Pictured on page 73.)

> 4 hard-boiled eggs, peeled and diced
> 1 hard-boiled egg, yolk only
> 6 to 8 tablespoons mayonnaise (plus
>   more if needed), divided
> 1/4 teaspoon dry mustard
> 1 teaspoon lemon juice
> Salt and pepper, to taste
> Dash of Tabasco
> Unsalted butter, softened
> Fresh chives, snipped, for optional
>   garnish

Remove five yolks and place them in a mixing bowl. Mash well with a fork. Add 4 tablespoons mayonnaise, dry mustard, lemon juice, salt and pepper, and Tabasco, mixing until smooth and not too runny. If necessary, add more mayonnaise. Finely chop the egg whites and mix together with the yolks. Lightly spread the filling on one slice of buttered bread. Top with another piece, butter side down. Trim crusts, and cut as desired. Optional: Brush one edge of each sandwich with mayonnaise, and dip in finely chopped parsley.

Makes enough filling for approximately 10 regular sandwiches.

Simple Simon Cake

(Pictured on page 77.)

Here's a cake everyone likes. It takes only minutes to prepare if you use your food processor. Perfect for the kids as an after-school treat, it works equally well for a fast weekend breakfast or tea cake.

> 1/4 cup plus 2 tablespoons butter, divided
> 3/4 cup granulated sugar
> 1 large egg
> 1/2 cup milk
> 1/2 teaspoon vanilla or almond extract
> 1 cup all-purpose flour
> 1 teaspoon baking soda
> 1/2 teaspoon salt
> Powdered sugar
> 1/2 teaspoon cinnamon, optional

Preheat the oven to 400° F., and grease a 9-inch-square baking pan.

Cut 1/4 cup butter into chunks. Using the metal blade of your processor, process the butter and sugar for 15 to 20 seconds until creamy. Add the egg, and process for 30 seconds to blend.

Turn on the processor, and slowly add the milk and vanilla through the feed tube. Turn off and scrape the sides of the bowl. Turn on to blend.

Add the flour, baking soda, and salt. Process with on-off bursts until well mixed.

Pour batter into the pan, and bake for 20 minutes, or until golden brown.

Cut the remaining 2 tablespoons butter into slivers onto the surface of the warm cake. With a knife, spread the butter over the top. Sift powdered sugar over the surface. For a spicy taste, add cinnamon to the powdered sugar before sifting.

Makes nine, 3-inch servings.

P-Nut Butter Surprise

This is a perfect recipe for nursery school tea and a favorite of adults, although they may not be willing to admit it. These nutritious snacks make a fun kitchen project for tiny fingers and grown-up hands.

BASIC RECIPE
1 cup creamy-style peanut butter
1 to 1½ cups non-fat dry milk
¾ to 1 cup honey

SURPRISES
M&M candies
Chocolate chips
Chocolate or carob-coated raisins
Whole peanuts

COATINGS
Crushed cereals
Finely ground nuts
Melted chocolate

Place the peanut butter, dry milk, and honey in a mixing bowl. Blend the ingredients together with your hands. Taste and modify the sweetness or texture by adding more honey or more dry milk.

To make candy, take a walnut-sized piece of dough, and roll it into a ball with your hands. Or, if you wish to add a surprise in the middle, take an M&M or chocolate chip and roll the ball around it. Set aside on a platter, and repeat until all the dough is used.

To add variety, roll some of the peanut butter balls in crushed cereal or chopped nuts.

If you wish to dip the balls in chocolate, it's best to chill the balls in the refrigerator for 30 minutes. Store any that aren't gobbled right up in an air-tight container in the refrigerator or freezer.

(Note that in the freezer the chocolate-coated candies will lose their sheen.)

Makes 3 dozen candies (give or take a few taste-tests).

Sunshine Sandwich

Here's a nutritious sandwich to brighten anyone's day.

1 peeled hard-boiled egg
2 teaspoons mayonnaise or sandwich
   dressing
¼ teaspoon prepared mustard
Salt and pepper, to taste
1 slice whole wheat bread, cut with a
   sunshine cookie cutter
1 small carrot, peeled and sliced in
   ¼-inch pieces

Remove the yolk and place it in a small bowl. Mash well with a fork and add the mayonnaise, mustard, and salt and pepper, mixing until smooth. If necessary, add more mayonnaise. Chop the egg white and mix together with the yolk. Lightly spread half the filling on the bread. With a sharp paring knife, slice the ¼-inch carrot pieces into triangles to fit the cut bread. Take the remaining egg spread and mound it in the center.

Makes 1 sandwich.

Sunshine Sandwich, Simple Simon Cake (recipe on page 75), and P-Nut Butter Surprise.

Willowdale Apple Crisp with Earl's Cream

This adaptation of an American classic features crisp, tart apples with orange and lemon zest, chopped dates, and a splash of Grand Marnier. The topping uses Earl Grey tea as a flavoring that delicately scents the whipped cream.

EARL'S CREAM
1 cup heavy cream, divided
1 tablespoon Earl Grey tea leaves
2 tablespoons plus 2 teaspoons
    granulated sugar, divided
½ teaspoon vanilla

APPLE CRISP
6 tart baking apples, peeled, cored,
    and sliced into 16 pieces each
1 tablespoon water
2 tablespoons granulated sugar
½ teaspoon ground cinnamon
1 cup chopped dates
1 teaspoon grated lemon rind
1 teaspoon grated orange rind
3 to 4 tablespoons orange-flavored
    liqueur
¾ cup brown sugar
1 cup sifted flour
¼ teaspoon salt
½ cup (1 stick) chilled, unsalted
    butter, cut into small pieces

To make the Earl's Cream, combine ½ cup heavy cream, tea leaves, and 2 tablespoons of sugar in a heavy-bottomed saucepan. Over medium-low heat, whisk the ingredients until blended. Stirring often, heat the mixture until it is steaming and begins to bubble around the edges.

Remove from heat, and cool to room temperature on a wire rack. Strain the mixture through a fine sieve to remove tea leaves. Cover and chill for several hours.

In the bowl of an electric mixer, combine the chilled tea mixture, the remaining ½ cup heavy cream, the remaining 2 teaspoons sugar, and the vanilla. Whip until cream forms firm peaks, and chill until serving.

To make the Apple Crisp, preheat the oven to 350° F. Grease an 8-inch-square baking dish or casserole dish.

In a 2-quart saucepan, combine the apples and water over medium heat. Sprinkle the sugar and cinnamon over the apples. Cook the apple mixture, tossing often, until the apples are partially cooked, about 10 minutes. Remove from heat and stir in the dates, grated lemon and orange rinds, and liqueur. Spoon the mixture into the greased baking dish.

In a mixing bowl, combine the brown sugar, flour, salt, and butter with a pastry blender, or your fingers, until the mixture is crumbly. Sprinkle over the apple mixture.

Bake Apple Crisp for 35 minutes. Just before removing the dish, turn the oven to broil. Place the Crisp 4 inches under the heat until the top is golden. (This doesn't take long so be sure and watch it.) Serve warm with Earl's Cream.

Makes 8 servings.

Willowdale Apple Crisp with Earl's Cream and a cup of Amanda's Tea Blend (recipe on page 45).

Moroccan Mint Sorbet

Reminiscent of the traditional sweet mint tea served after a North African meal, this bracing sorbet is a palate cleanser as well as a delicious dessert.

4 cups water
1 tablespoon Gunpowder or Pearl
   Dew green tea
½ cup chopped fresh mint leaves
½ cup granulated sugar
Mint leaves for garnish

In a saucepan, bring the water to a boil. Add the tea and mint, and let stand 5 minutes to infuse. Strain into another container, blend in the sugar, and chill.

   Place the chilled mixture in your ice cream maker and follow manufacturer's instructions. If you don't have an ice cream maker, you can freeze the tea mixture in ice cube trays. Just before serving, process the mint sorbet in a food processor until it looks finely grained.

   Scoop the sorbet into wine glasses, and garnish with a mint sprig.

Makes 1 quart.

Cardamom Tea Cream with Orange Sauce

Tea is not often thought of as a flavoring for food, but it can add a subtle touch to many dishes. For an unusual finale to your next dinner party, try serving this simple-to-make tea cream in your favorite set of demitasse cups. With its lingering taste of tea and cardamom, this elegant dessert will surprise your most exotic guest.

1 cup heavy cream, divided
3 tablespoons English Breakfast or
　Darjeeling tea leaves
4 crushed cardamom pods
⅓ cup granulated sugar
Pinch of salt
1½ teaspoons unflavored gelatin
1½ cups sour cream

ORANGE SAUCE
1 cup fresh orange juice
½ cup honey
2 teaspoons grated orange rind
Orange zest for garnish

In a heavy-bottomed saucepan, combine ¾ cup heavy cream, tea, lightly crushed cardamom pods, sugar, and salt. Over medium-low heat, whisk the ingredients until blended. Stirring often, heat until mixture just begins to boil.

Remove from heat, and allow cream to cool for 15 minutes until it reaches room temperature.

In a small bowl, combine the remaining ¼ cup heavy cream and gelatin. Let stand for 10 minutes, then heat in a microwave or small saucepan over medium-low heat until the gelatin dissolves and the mixture is hot, but not boiling. Set aside.

In a large bowl, whisk the sour cream until smooth. Pour the tea mixture and the gelatin mixture through a sieve into the sour cream. Stir until smooth and well blended. Pour into small dessert cups, and chill for several hours.

To make sauce, combine the orange juice and honey in a saucepan. Cook over medium-low heat, stirring constantly with a wooden spoon until the mixture is reduced by half. Remove from heat. Strain mixture, and stir in the orange rind. Cool and chill until ready to use.

To serve, pour a small amount of orange sauce over the top of each dessert cup, and garnish with orange zest.

Makes 4 servings.

Pineapple Macadamia Upside-Down Cake

Pineapple Upside-Down Cake has always been one of those down-home comfort foods. With the addition of toasted Macadamia nuts, this simple sponge cake becomes a tropical treat.

TOPPING
6 tablespoons butter
½ cup brown sugar, firmly packed
1 can (20 ounces) sliced pineapple, drained
¾ cup toasted macadamia nuts, coarsely chopped (see Note)

SPONGE CAKE
1 cup all-purpose flour
1¼ teaspoons baking powder
¼ teaspoon salt
4 eggs, separated
¾ cup granulated sugar
1 teaspoon vanilla
¼ cup milk

Whipped cream for garnish
Macadamia nuts, toasted and finely chopped for garnish

Preheat the oven to 350° F.

To make topping, melt the butter in a heavy, 10-inch skillet over low heat. Tip and swirl the skillet so that the butter coats the sides of the pan. Remove from heat, and spread the brown sugar evenly over the bottom of the skillet. Cover the sugar with sliced pineapple, placing the first slice in the center of the skillet. Sprinkle the chopped macadamia nuts over the pineapple-sugar mixture. Set aside.

To make sponge cake, sift together the flour, baking powder, and salt. Set aside.

In the bowl of an electric mixer, combine the egg yolks and sugar. Beat until light and lemony in color. Beat in the vanilla. With the mixer on low speed, slowly add the sifted flour mixture and milk until completely blended. In a clean bowl, whip the egg whites until stiff, but not dry, and fold into the flour mixture. Pour the cake batter into the prepared skillet, spreading the batter evenly over the topping. Bake for 35 to 40 minutes until the cake is golden and springs back with the touch of a fingertip. Immediately invert on a serving platter, and allow to cool 15 minutes before serving.

To serve, garnish each cake slice with a large dollop of whipped cream, dusted heavily with the finely chopped macadamia nuts.

Makes 6 to 8 servings.

Note: To toast macadamia nuts, *preheat the oven to 350° F., and spread the nuts on a baking sheet. Bake for 5 minutes. With a wooden spoon, stir the nuts to insure even browning. Continue to bake nuts another 5 minutes, checking to make sure they do not burn.*

Three Berry Shortcake with Strawberry Sauce & Summer Cream

Here's dessert at its best: sun-ripened berries, home-made strawberry sauce and whipped cream seasoned with the scent of summer roses.

1 quart small strawberries
1 quart raspberries
1 quart blueberries

STRAWBERRY SAUCE
4 cups sliced strawberries
¾ cup powdered sugar
2 teaspoons lemon juice

SUMMER CREAM
½ pint heavy cream
2 teaspoons granulated sugar
1 teaspoon rose water (see Note)

SHORTCAKE DOUGH
2 cups all-purpose flour
2 tablespoons granulated sugar
1 tablespoon baking powder
½ teaspoon salt
½ cup chilled unsalted butter, cut
   into pieces
⅔ cup milk
1 egg, slightly beaten

In a bowl, combine the strawberries, raspberries, and blueberries. Set aside at room temperature.

To make strawberry sauce, place the sliced strawberries, powdered sugar, and lemon juice in a food processor and puree. Set aside. (Makes approximately 2 cups.)

To make summer cream, whip the heavy cream until soft peaks form. Add the granulated sugar and rose water, and continue to whip until stiff peaks just begin to form. Cover and chill.

Preheat the oven to 425° F.

To make the shortcakes, sift together the flour, sugar, baking powder, and salt in a large bowl. Cut the chilled butter into the dry ingredients until the mixture resembles coarse crumbs. Combine the milk and egg, and add to the flour mixture. Stir until the mixture just forms a dough.

Dust hands with flour and knead the dough gently on a lightly floured surface two or three times. (Handling the dough roughly or too much will keep it from rising properly.) Pat out 1 inch thick, and cut into shapes, using a biscuit cutter or a knife. Place on an ungreased baking sheet and bake for 10 to 12 minutes until golden.

To assemble topping, pour ½ cup of strawberry sauce, ¼ cup at a time, into the whipped cream, using a rubber spatula to make a swirling pattern. Leave some "ribbons" of jam visible.

To assemble the dessert, split each hot shortcake with a fork, and spread 1 tablespoon of the sauce over each half. Spoon the berries over each cake, and cover generously with Summer Cream.

Makes 6 to 8 shortcakes.

Note: *Rose water can be found in the liquor department of your supermarket or gourmet specialty market.*

Variation: For a low-fat alternative, substitute low fat lemon yogurt for the whipped cream and rose water mixture.

Cashew Shortbread (recipe on page 63) and Jasmine Ice Cream.

Jasmine Ice Cream

This delicately scented ice cream has a refreshing flavor that will accompany almost any meal, and make it memorable.

> **2 cups heavy cream**
> **2 cups milk**
> **2 rounded tablespoons loose Jasmine**
>   **tea leaves**
> **½ cup granulated sugar**
> **Pinch of salt**

In a heavy-bottomed saucepan, combine the heavy cream, milk, tea leaves, sugar, and salt. Whisk the ingredients over medium-low heat until blended, and heat until the mixture just begins to boil, stirring often.

Remove from heat, and cool to room temperature on a wire rack. Cover and chill the mixture for 6 hours or overnight.

Strain the mixture through a fine sieve to remove tea leaves. Place the chilled mixture in your ice cream maker and follow manufacturer's instructions.

Makes 1 quart.

Blackberry & Lime Curd Tartlets

The combination of blackberry and lime curds gives these tartlets a snappy and distinctive flavor.

PÂTE SUCRÉE
2½ cups all-purpose flour
⅓ cup granulated sugar
1 cup (2 sticks) cold, unsalted butter
2 egg yolks
2 to 3 tablespoons ice water

BLACKBERRY CURD (see Note)
3 cups blackberries
6 tablespoons unsalted butter
3 tablespoons granulated sugar
2 tablespoons lemon juice
3 large eggs
2 egg yolks

LIME CURD (see Note)
6 egg yolks, beaten
1 cup granulated sugar
½ cup fresh lime juice
½ cup (1 stick) unsalted butter, cut
  into small pieces
1 tablespoon grated lime zest

Blackberries for garnish

To make pastry, put the flour and sugar in the bowl of your food processor. Cut butter into small pieces, and add. Process until the mixture looks like coarse meal. Add the yolks. With the machine running, add the ice water, one tablespoon at a time, until the dough is one mass on the blade. Turn out onto a piece of plastic wrap. Flatten into a disc and wrap. Chill for 1 hour.

To make tartlets, preheat the oven to 350° F. Spray tartlet forms with cooking spray. Roll out dough, cut, and press into forms. Trim edges with a knife, and press rim to form. Freeze the shells for 15 minutes. Prick the bottoms with a fork, and bake for 12 to 15 minutes until golden. Let cool completely before filling.

To make blackberry curd, puree the berries and pass through a strainer or food mill to remove seeds. In a saucepan, heat the blackberry puree and butter, stirring constantly until the butter has melted. Add the sugar and lemon juice, and continue to cook until the sugar has dissolved.

Put the eggs and yolks in a bowl and whisk to mix. Slowly blend in some of the hot puree. Return the egg/blackberry mixture to the saucepan and continue to cook, constantly stirring, until the mixture reaches 170° F., and is pudding thick. Chill. (Makes about 2 cups.)

To make lime curd, strain the yolks through a sieve into a medium saucepan. Add the sugar and juice, and cook over low heat, stirring constantly, for about 15 minutes, until the mixture thickens and coats the back of a wooden spoon. Remove from heat, and stir until mixture cools a bit. Stir in the butter, piece by piece, until it is fully incorporated. Add the zest. Cool completely and chill. (Makes about 2 cups.)

To make tartlets, spoon (or use a pastry bag) the two curds into the baked tart shells, making designs or patterns. Garnish with berries.

Makes twelve 2½- to 3-inch tartlets.

Note: Curds can be made ahead of time and kept refrigerated for several days before being spooned into tartlet shells.

Good Luck Fortune Cookies

Here's your chance to be prophetic. While these cookies take time and patience, you have the delightful opportunity to predict the future or give away a secret.

> 2 large egg whites
> ½ cup powdered sugar
> 3 tablespoons butter, melted and cooled
> ⅓ cup sifted all-purpose flour
> 1 tablespoon Grand Marnier
> Grated zest of ½ small orange
> Homemade fortunes to your liking, optional

Preheat the oven to 375° F.

In the mixing bowl of an electric mixer, whisk the egg whites until foamy. Slowly add the powdered sugar, and continue to whisk until double in size, but not until peaks form. Stir in the melted butter, flour, Grand Marnier, and grated orange zest.

Using a non-stick or well-oiled baking sheet, spoon out 3 teaspoonfuls of batter on the sheet. Using a blunt knife or spatula, thinly spread the batter into a rectangle, 1½ inches by 3 inches, as evenly as possible. Repeat for a second cookie. (It's best to make only 2 or 3 cookies at a time because the cookies become brittle as they cool and you will need to work very fast.) Bake for 5 to 7 minutes, or until the cookies brown around the edges. (You'll need to watch the first batch carefully to determine the correct time for your oven.)

Remove cookies from oven. Immediately slip a spatula under the first cookie. Lift the cookie and roll it lengthwise around a chopstick, pencil, or wooden spoon. Slide off pencil and onto a wire rack to cool. (Have a bowl of ice water close by to keep your fingertips cool. These cookies are hot when you roll them.) Repeat for the other cookies. Store in an airtight container. Before serving, slip a fortune into the hollow center.

Makes approximately 18 cookies.

Variation: Substitute raspberry syrup for Grand Marnier, and ½ teaspoon grated lemon zest for the grated zest of ½ a small orange. Proceed as directed. Note: Raspberry syrup is available at most supermarkets. Speciality grocery stores carry the Italian syrup, Torani, which works well.

General Index

Recipe Index

Credits

Page 3, Donut-shaped tea service by
Joan Takayama-Ogawa.

Page 4, Contemporary tea set by
Marek Cecula.

Page 6, Revival tea set by Salins
Studio, France.

Page 20, Organic tea set by Lynne
Turner.

Page 73, Tea cup, sugar, creamer, and
plate by Mikasa China.

Acknowledgments

Once again, thanks go to my friends, who generously shared their ideas, time, recipes, photographic props, and memorable poems, especially Lisa Shara Hall, Larry Kirkland, Linda Crumb, Marcia Morgan, Pete Petersen, Karen Brooks, Myrthle Griffin, Monique Siu, Patty Merrill, Amanda Baines Ashley, Jan Edwards, Margot Barnett, Anita Sande, Marie Hein, Ben Alaoui, Marrakesh Restaurant, Alexandra's The Design Source, June Moriyasu Soshu and the WAKAI Tea School in Portland, Oregon. Thanks also go to Catherine Gleason, my editor and a great tea-drinking partner, who kindles writing as rich and full-bodied as my favorite Assam. To Ed Gowans, photographer, whose competent skill and warmhearted kindness made working in the studio a pleasure. To Sam McKean, food stylist, whose keen eye, calm nature, and technique in the kitchen were invaluable. And, to Judith Rose, production manager, designer, and friend, who kept us all in line with helpful advice and the best Yogi tea I'll ever taste.

A special thanks to Starbuck's Tea Master, Steven Smith, who opened his door and his knowledge with great generosity. And, it goes without saying, to Bill LeBlond, senior editor at Chronicle Books, who, like the subject of this book, is always able to stimulate, relax, tantalize, and cheer his writers to their best.